THE WORLD OF SCIENCE

DISEASE AND MEDICINE

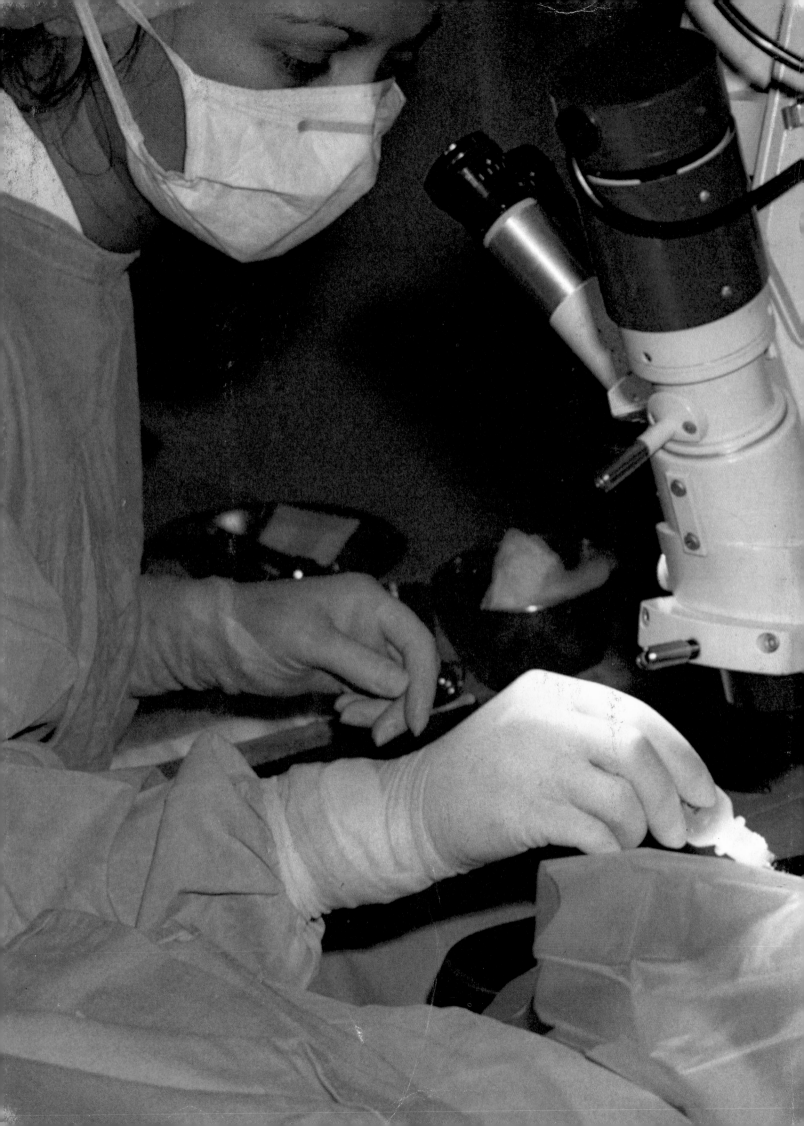

THE WORLD OF SCIENCE

DISEASE AND MEDICINE

IRENE FEKETE &
PETER DORRINGTON WARD

Facts On File Publications
New York, New York • Bicester, England

DISEASE AND MEDICINE

Copyright © Macdonald & Co (Publishers) Ltd
1985, 1987

First published in the United States of America in
1985 by Facts on File, Inc., 460 Park Avenue South,
New York, N.Y.10016

First published in Great Britain in 1985 by Orbis
Publishing Limited, London

**Library of Congress Cataloging in Publication
Data**

Main entry under title:

World of Science

   Includes index.
   Summary: A twenty-five volume encyclopedia of
scientific subjects, designed for eight- to twelve-year-
olds. One volume is entirely devoted to projects.
   1. Science—Dictionaries, Juvenile.   1. Science—
Dictionaries
Q121.J86   1984   500   84-1654

ISBN: 0-8160-1060-9

Printed in Yugoslavia
10 9 8 7 6 5 4 3 2

Consultant editors
Eleanor Felder, former managing editor, *Scientific
American*
James Neujahr, Dean of the School of Education, City
College of New York
Ethan Signer, Professor of Biology, Massachusetts
Institute of Technology
J. Tuzo Wilson, Director General, Ontario Science
Centre

Previous pages An
eye operation in
progress. The surgeon
works looking through
a special type of
microscope to get a
better view of the tiny
area on which he is
operating.

Editor Penny Clarke
Designer Roger Kohn

CONTENTS

Note There are some unusual words in this book. They are explained in the Glossary on page 62. The first time each word is used in the text it is printed in *italics*.

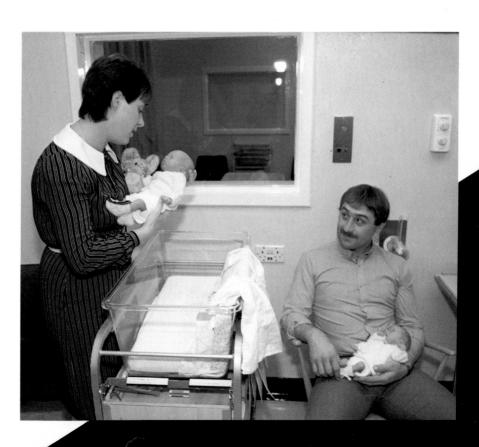

► Thanks to modern screening techniques (page 54) these parents may have known they were to have twins

I INTRODUCTION

TALKING ABOUT HEALTH

Most of us enjoy visiting a foreign country. We like seeing how other people live. At first, we notice only how different everything seems. We soon discover that no matter where we go, people like to talk about the same things. Adults swap stories about jobs and families. Children talk about school, games and hobbies. But everyone at every age talks about health in one way or another.

We say we feel healthy when our body is working so smoothly we don't think about it. We enjoy exercise and food, sleep well and keep up mentally and physically with others of our own age. When something goes wrong and we cannot do these things we say we are ill. It is miserable to wake up with a sore throat or pain in the stomach. This can mean missing out on something important at

school or at home. Some of us remember when a doctor or nurse pierced our arm with a big needle. We were told that the jab would protect us from some serious illness. We know about wounds and accidents too. A girl hurriedly cleaning some knives may cut her finger badly. A boy, climbing a tree, slips and tumbles to the ground. One leg twists under him in an awkward way and hurts so much he cannot move. The bone inside the leg has been broken. A doctor will put the leg back into its correct position then cover it with white plaster so that it stays straight and still while the bone heals.

Continuing an ancient tradition
Adults talk about health more often than children. Often they use special names for illnesses or *treatments*. The words may

congenital club foot, cleft palate		
inherited blood diseases, colour blindness, low intelligence		
acquired	**bacteria** tuberculosis, cholera, lock jaw, plague, typhoid	
	viruses mumps, influenza, common cold, measles, chickenpox	
	fungi athlete's foot, thrush	
	protozoa malaria, liver fluke, amebic dysentery, tapeworm	
	traumatic	*physical* sunburn, bone breaks and fractures, wounds
		chemical lead poisoning, acid burns, insecticide poisoning, mercury poisoning
	diseases of old age osteoarthritis, varicose veins, arteriosclerosis, Parkinson's disease	
	diseases of poor nutrition anemia, scurvy	
	bodily malfunction diabetes, overactive thyroid gland	

▲ We can be ill in many ways. Congenital and inherited diseases are those we are born with. The first group happen if a baby is damaged in some way as it grows inside its mother's body. The second group come from the child's parents and are passed down from one generation to the next. Most diseases are acquired. Some occur when tiny harmful living things we usually call germs get into the body. There are many types of germ: bacteria, viruses, fungi, protozoa. Wounds and accidents are called traumatic illnesses. Other types of illnesses come with old age as the body gradually wears out, or because the body does not get the right kind of food or because one of the parts of the body does not work properly.

6

seem odd and difficult but they are important because people must be precise when describing illnesses. Many names for diseases and treatments come from Greek or Latin. This is because for many centuries Greek and Latin were the languages used for scientific writing in most Western countries. Today's medical vocabulary still reflects this ancient tradition. New discoveries and cures are usually given names based on Greek or Latin terms.

Television, radio, newspapers and magazines are full of news about health. People are intensely interested in medical discoveries. They want to know how to live more healthy lives. They want to hear about successes in treating diseases everyone fears, such as cancer. In many countries around the world, governments too take action to help citizens stay healthy and provide for those who are ill. Nations also co-operate with each other to save lives when disasters like floods or earthquakes happen. Gradually people everywhere are beginning to live longer and some diseases that used to kill millions are being wiped out. In some places, though, increasing good health and a larger population in its turn brings new medical problems.

◀ An American couple are jogging while a doctor watches and times their speed. Later he will examine them to see what effect exercise has on them. Taking regular exercise is an increasingly popular way to keep healthy.

▲ Women and children in Nigeria are being visited by a doctor sent to them by the Red Cross. The Red Cross is an intenational body that sends medical help quickly to many parts of the world when there is an emergency caused by a natural disaster or war.

WHAT IS MEDICINE?

Slowly, over thousands of years, people have been collecting medical knowledge, information about what makes us ill, what can make us better, and what can keep us healthy. Medicine is the science of preventing and curing disease. It is a huge and constantly expanding body of knowledge. Today there are many different types of doctor and medical *specialist* because no one person, however brilliant, can be an expert in all the branches of medicine. It often takes a team of specialists to care for someone who is seriously ill. Many diseases affect different parts of the body at once so the specialists' knowledge helps in planning and carrying out the right treatment.

The key to medical knowledge is understanding the human body, how it works when it is healthy and what happens when it is attacked by disease or is injured. Human beings have been puzzling over how their bodies work for centuries. Surprisingly enough, even today, we still do not have all the answers. Some of the internal parts of the body are so tiny we have seen them for the first time only recently, thanks to powerful microscopes, cameras and new machines. Some of the important *chemicals*, like those in the brain, have been discovered only in the past ten

years. How they act is still a mystery. The same is true of many illnesses that cause great pain and suffering. Others have been explained and doctors can prevent or cure them. New instruments, new machines, new tests and new experiments help medical researchers collect more facts about health and disease. These facts are pieced together and form clues leading to greater knowledge and successful cures.

Sometimes when we are impressed by a new medical triumph we forget that even the most highly-trained modern doctor has a great deal in common with doctors long ago. He or she begins any attempt to help a sick person by asking detailed questions about their general health and the sort of life they lead. The doctor then makes a very careful physical *examination*. A doctor can discover a great deal about your health just by looking closely at your body, finding out how warm or cold you are, noticing how fast or slowly your heart is beating, how you are breathing and how you move. The questions are to find out about things the doctor cannot see. In the past doctors had just a few simple instruments to help their eyes and hands make this examination. Now they have special lights, complicated instruments, machines and tests, but the basic examination is much the same.

▼ When we are ill, we may need the help of several experts. **(Below left)** A girl is having her chest examined by X-rays. These are special rays that make it possible to take a picture of what is happening inside the body without cutting into it. **(Below right)** A team of doctors is preparing to operate, that is, cut into a sick person. They may remove some part of the body that is no longer working properly or they may repair some damage a disease has done. The doctor on the right has a special job. He is measuring the exact amount of gases, especially oxygen, the patient breathes in to be put into a deep, painless and safe sleep.

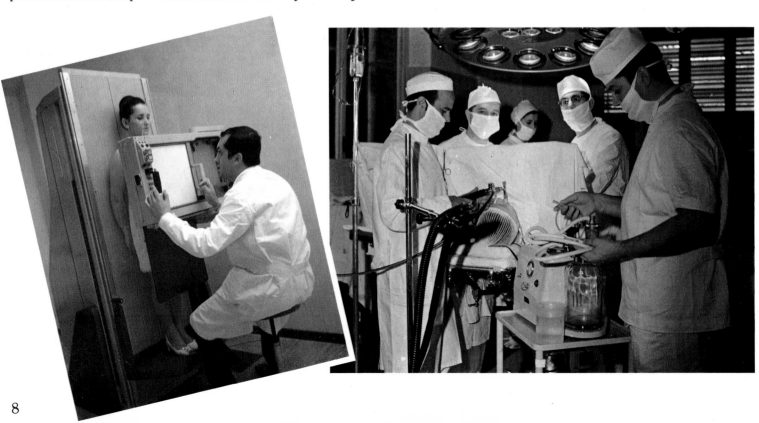

Making a diagnosis

The next step a doctor takes is to make a *diagnosis* – that is to decide which illness a patient has. This may be obvious in the case of a deep cut or some accident. But many illnesses can have very similar effects on our bodies at first. What would be helpful to cure one disease could make another worse. This is why correct diagnosis is so important and much of a doctor's training is designed to help him or her make this decision quickly and accurately. A good medical diagnosis must take into account everything that might be happening in your body to produce the *symptoms* you feel, and often requires tests before the doctor can be quite certain.

When a diagnosis has been made, treatment will begin. medical treatment can take many forms. Sometimes a doctor

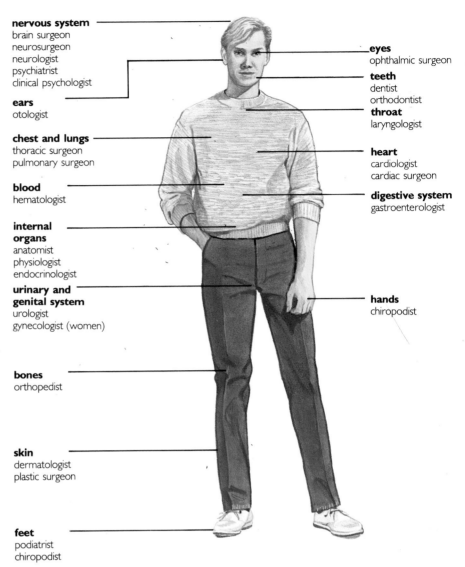

nervous system
brain surgeon
neurosurgeon
neurologist
psychiatrist
clinical psychologist

ears
otologist

chest and lungs
thoracic surgeon
pulmonary surgeon

blood
hematologist

internal organs
anatomist
physiologist
endocrinologist

urinary and genital system
urologist
gynecologist (women)

bones
orthopedist

skin
dermatologist
plastic surgeon

feet
podiatrist
chiropodist

eyes
ophthalmic surgeon

teeth
dentist
orthodontist

throat
laryngologist

heart
cardiologist
cardiac surgeon

digestive system
gastroenterologist

hands
chiropodist

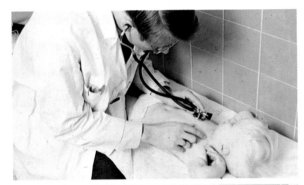

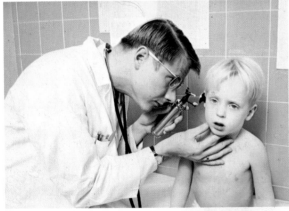

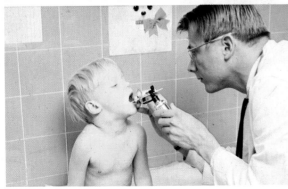

knows that the body can heal itself quickly provided a person stays warm and quiet in bed. For other illnesses a patient may need special food or some special substance to help the body recover. Sometimes a part of the body may be so injured or diseased, it must be removed quickly. Before, during, and after treatment a doctor will re-examine a patient to check that the treatment is working correctly and that good health is returning.

▲ This chart gives a good idea of some of the main types of modern specialists who care for our health. Other specialists study the problems and illnesses we may have at a certain time of life. A pediatrician, for example, specializes in caring for babies and young children. A geriatrician specializes in the care of the elderly.

◄ A doctor is carefully examining a child's heart (**top**), ears (**middle**) and throat (**bottom**). In each case he has a special instrument to help him. He listens to the child's heart and breathing through a stethoscope. He uses an otoscope with a powerful small light to help him see into the child's ears and throat.

9

MEDICINE IN THE PAST: EGYPT, GREECE AND ROME

With the help of historians we can discover what people long ago thought about disease and how they tried to conquer it. By examining ancient *skeletons*, looking at pictures painted in caves, in tombs and on pottery, as well as by reading ancient books, we see that people slowly came to understand that illness was not the work of evil spirits. At first, because people had so little knowledge of how their bodies worked, they usually assumed illness was the curse of a god or an enemy. About 3800 years ago, the Egyptians made a significant move from magic to medicine. Their doctors wrote down precise descriptions of diseases and then worked out combinations of substances that

▼ This ancient Egyptian papyrus, dating from about 1200 BC gives a 'cure' for headache – or half-head as the Egyptians called it. Among other things, the sufferer had to recite some special words over a clay model of a crocodile.

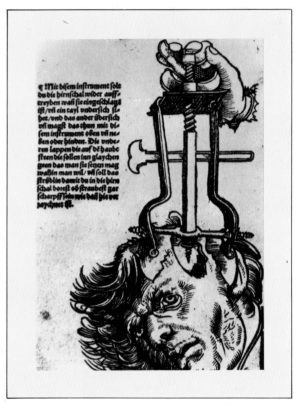

▲ Brain surgery is not new, even though the methods may have changed! This diagram comes from a 16th-century medical textbook. It shows an operation to relieve pressure from injuries or illnesses that caused fluid to build up inside the skull. Or, as people believed, to release evil spirits. Amazingly the patients sometimes survived these operations, because archaeologists have found skulls that show signs of healing.

brought relief. They wrote on papyrus, a kind of paper made from reeds that grow along the banks of the river Nile. Preserved in the hot, dry sands of Egypt these writings survived and we can study them today. They are the oldest medical records in the world. They tell us that

even so long ago doctors understood that a person's heart beat was an important clue to his state of health. They explain that many herbs, small plants that grew wild in the countryside, contained substances that could cure. One of these early medical records advises doctors to put fresh willow leaves on any wound that would not heal. Today, many drugs contain a powerful healing substance extracted from willow leaves.

▲ The ancient theatre at the healing sanctuary of Epidaurus in Greece was part of the cure. Doctors believed that watching plays about strong emotions helped people get well. Today modern medicine sometimes uses drama and dance to help people suffering from mental illness.

Hippocrates – the Father of Medicine

The ancient Greeks, 2400 years ago, made great progress in medicine. Hippocrates, who came from the island of Kos, is called the Father of Medicine. His writings, and those of his best students, were used as the standard medical textbooks for many centuries.

Hippocrates taught that a doctor had to observe his patient very carefully before he made a diagnosis. He taught that good food and a restful atmosphere were important aids to curing any illness. He

believed very strongly that all doctors should be properly trained and should be people their patients could trust. He drew up an oath, which was named after him, to be taken by his pupils. In some medical schools this Hippocratic Oath is still recited by new doctors as part of the ceremony when they become fully qualified. Its phrases may sound strange to us because Hippocrates calls on the ancient gods to witness what he says, but the ideals of his oath are as important to

▲ Asclepius, the Greek god of healing, is shown treating a patient with a wounded arm in this sculpture dating from the 4th century BC.

► Although Hippocrates lived over 4000 years ago, many of his ideas about medicine and the way doctors should treat their patients are still followed. It is not surprising that he is called the 'Father of Medicine'.

good medical practice today as they were so many centuries ago. In the oath, a doctor promises that he will use his skill only to help and never harm his patients. He also promises to keep secret anything he learns from a patient, either while he is treating him or at any other time.

► The Romans understood the importance of good supplies of fresh water for their towns and cities. If necessary, they built huge aqueducts – bridges to carry water – to take water to the cities. This is the aqueduct at Spoleto.

Hippocrates' ideas spread
Greek doctors trained by Hippocrates and his disciples spread the ideas of early scientific medicine throughout the ancient world. When Greece was conquered by Rome, Greek doctors were taken to Rome and the Roman provinces as slaves of important men. Because of their skill, they often won both freedom and great respect. Their medical ideas influenced the Romans greatly, especially in matters of public health. The Romans thought it wise to spend money on things that would keep the whole community healthy and fit. Their doctors understood that many diseases came from what they called 'bad air' or 'bad water', although they did not know how this happened. They drained swamps and built tremendous *sewer* systems and waterworks so their cities could be healthy places in which to live. Some of those structures are still in use.

CHANGING CIRCUMSTANCES AND CHANGING IDEAS

For hundreds of years after the work of the Greeks and Romans, medicine appeared to make little progress. As the great Roman empire collapsed, cities, towns and villages were devastated by wars and invasions. The survivors, living in ruins, took less and less care about keeping themselves and their homes clean. When good water, drainage systems and public baths broke down, there were no longer any trained engineers to repair them or build new ones. There was no central government to enforce laws to protect public health. Diseases that thrive in dirt and bad water spread rapidly.

A curse from God?

The worst of these, the Great Plague or Black Death, first appeared in Europe in 1347. It came from China, carried by fleas that lived on the black rats infesting ships and warehouses. It spread quickly inland from the ports and harbours and soon huge numbers of people were dying in agony. Historians estimate that over one third of the population of Europe died in about three years. At first, no one could understand how people caught it. It seemed to attack the young and healthy as well as the old and frail. It carried off

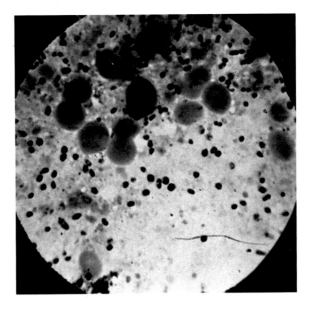

rich and poor alike. Some people thought it was a curse from God. Doctors could do little for their patients and often caught the disease themselves. Then they began to notice that people who kept themselves and their houses very clean and avoided touching plague victims often escaped. They worked out that plague was a *contagious* disease, one that is spread from person to person by close physical contact.

When this much was understood cities like Venice made laws to keep out anyone who had been near a person suffering the

◀ Today, through a modern microscope, we can take a picture of the deadly germs that caused the Great Plague. They are called *Pasteurella pestis*, named after the French scientist, Louis Pasteur who first discovered them. When they infect lymph glands and blood vessels, they cause bubonic plague. When they infect the lungs, they cause pneumonic plague which is spread from person to person by coughs and sneezes.

◀ Part of this 15th-century church is curtained off and turned into a hospital. The sick and injured are being cared for both by monks and ordinary people. Notice that all sorts of different wounds and diseases are being cared for in the same place and that not too much attention is paid to cleanliness. Even animals are allowed to wander in with the visitors.

plague or had been to a place where plague was widespread. People who had any contact with the plague were banned from Venice for forty days. That was the time it took from contact until the first signs of the disease appeared. This practice gives us our modern word 'quarantine' – from the Latin word meaning forty. Quarantine is a period of time, which may be from a few days to several months, when a person must be kept away from others if he or she has been in contact with a serious contagious disease. We have quarantine laws for animals too. They can *infect* human beings with several serious diseases, the most terrible being rabies, for which there is little hope of a cure.

Again and again, the plague returned to Europe and killed tens of thousands of people. By the end of the seventeenth century, improved medical understanding, as well as better standards of cleanliness, controlled it. Modern drugs have nearly conquered it. But in some remote parts of the world plague still claims victims today.

Monasteries and medicine

In the medieval monasteries, places where men and women lived lives dedicated to prayer and study, interest in scientific medicine remained alive. Monks and nuns copied the precious Greek and Roman medical texts. They also kept herb gardens to grow plants that were useful in remedies. Some monasteries and churches reserved a part of their buildings as special places to care for the sick. From this idea the modern hospital developed. One of the earliest, St Bartholomew's in London, was founded in 1123. It still exists today and is an important centre for medical *research*, the care of the sick and the training of new doctors and nurses.

Universities, too, grew up from the monasteries and church schools. The University of Padua in Italy became famous for its medical school. Scientists there revived the ancient practice of *dissection*, the careful cutting open of dead bodies. Through dissection, doctors in training can learn about the parts of the body beneath the skin and see what happens inside when a person dies of a specific illness.

The work of Vesalius

In 1543, Vesalius, a professor at Padua, published a book on the human body. His drawings were so accurate that they were used as the basis of medical studies for centuries. This new interest in the study of *anatomy*, the science of how the human body is made, and *physiology*, the science of how a living body works, marked the beginning of modern medical research.

► This illustration of a mandrake plant and its human-shaped root comes from a Greek medical text that describes how certain quantities of the ground-up root will cause sleep or vomiting. Books illustrated like this were often a doctor's most valuable possession.

► Many herbal preparations were sold to doctors from an apothecary's shop – the medieval equivalent of a chemist or druggist. This one in 15th-century Germany shows how the combinations of useful medicines were inscribed in a record book and the herbs and other substances stored in tightly closed china jars.

PIECES IN A JIGSAW – BLOOD AND GERMS

More than 400 years have passed since Vesalius published his book, *The Fabric of the Human Body*. Since then, medicine's fight against disease has been like a giant jigsaw puzzle that is being solved by a great many people around the world. At first, it was just doctors who fitted in the basic pieces. Then, gradually, other scientists, especially physicists and chemists began to help. As more and more pieces were added, the outlines became clearer and work could progress faster. Today research in many countries produces so much information that computers are needed to keep track of developments in major areas of medical research.

William Harvey and blood circulation

In the early stages things moved very slowly. In 1599, a young Englishman, William Harvey, travelled to the medical school at Padua to complete his studies. While he was there he realized how little was known about how a healthy living body worked, despite the pioneering work of Vesalius and others. When doctors in training examined a dead body they could not be sure, just by looking at some internal part, how it worked when the person was alive. Harvey became fascinated by the heart and the way blood moved inside our bodies. By carefully examining the tubes that carried blood to and from the heart in bodies he dissected, and by looking at veins close to the skin in living patients, he discovered that blood is constantly moving round, or circulating, within the body. The heart is in fact a pump. In 1628 Harvey published *On the movement of the heart and blood*, one of the most important medical books ever written and a vital piece in the medical jigsaw.

The first microscope

Not long after Harvey's discovery, a Dutchman, Anthon van Leeuwenhoek, who ground glass lenses for a living, experimented with them and invented the

▼ Today a doctor or scientist can use an endoscope (**below left**) to look directly into the human heart while it is working and observe exactly how the chambers pump the blood into the lungs to be purified and then out around the body again. They can also see how tiny tendons support the inner walls of the heart's four chambers (**below**). William Harvey had to work out what was happening by experiments on the outside of a body and compare this with what he discovered when he examined the heart of a dead man.

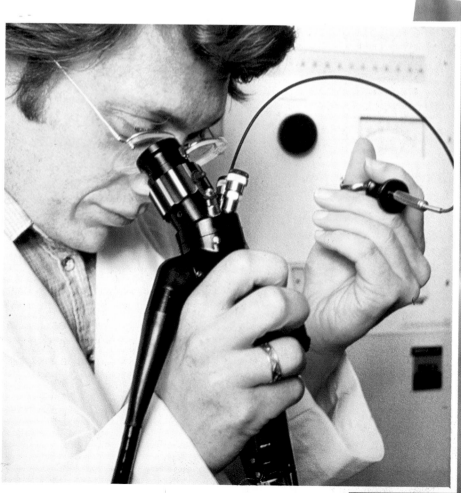

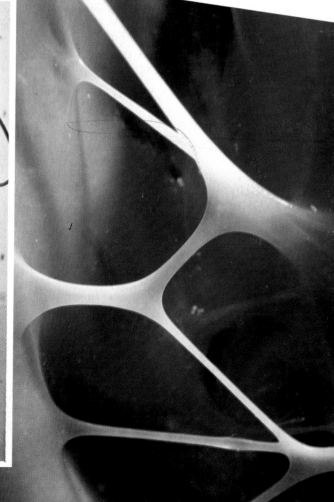

microscope, one of the most important instruments for any scientific research but especially for medicine. This tube containing magnifying lenses and mirrors to focus light suddenly made a previously invisible part of the world visible to us.

A NEW SCIENCE

Even the earliest, least powerful microscopes opened a window on the world of micro-organisms, the tiny living things that exist all around us – and inside us as well. Exploring that world and learning to distinguish between helpful and harmful micro-organisms and learning how to control and use them eventually became a new science – *bacteriology*. This science is named after *bacteria*, the most simple forms of life. Some bacteria living inside us help our bodies work. Millions live within our digestive tract helping to turn the food we eat into food we can absorb and use in the body. Some harmful bacteria are quickly

destroyed by our body's defence system so we stay healthy. Others are so powerful that unless we are perfectly fit and are protected by proper medical care, they can multiply within us and kill us quickly. Harmful bacteria are the kind we commonly call germs. But not all germs are bacteria, some are even more tiny things that seem to have some but not all the characteristics of a living thing. They are called *viruses*.

Doctors and scientists took a long time to fit bacteria and then viruses into the medical jigsaw. It was nearly 150 years after van Leeuwenhoek first looked into his simple microscope and saw tiny living things that doctors began to suspect that some of these things might play an important part in causing disease.

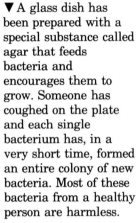

▼ A glass dish has been prepared with a special substance called agar that feeds bacteria and encourages them to grow. Someone has coughed on the plate and each single bacterium has, in a very short time, formed an entire colony of new bacteria. Most of these bacteria from a healthy person are harmless.

▼ As microscopes became more powerful, scientists could identify harmful bacteria more easily. In the **bottom** picture we can see the bacteria that cause a type of pneumonia, a serious disease that attacks our breathing and causes a high fever. In the picture **below** the same bacteria are magnified 40,000 times by an electron microscope.

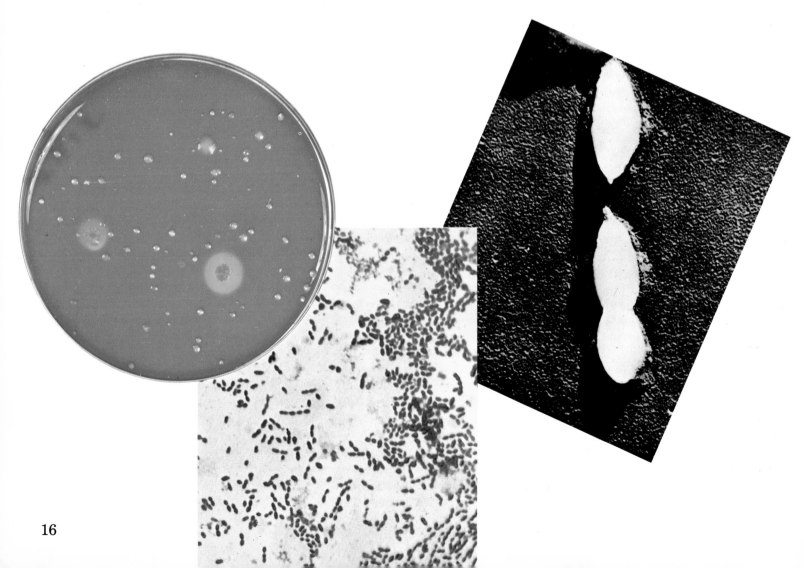

16

THE GERM THEORY OF DISEASE

One of the most important advances in the history of medicine happened because a French manufacturer of alcohol wanted to find out why his fermenting beet juice went sour. He took his problem to a distinguished research chemist, Louis Pasteur, who was a professor at Lille University. Pasteur examined many samples of the spoiled juice under a microscope. In the samples he saw thousands of micro-organisms. Tests and experiments convinced him that these micro-organisms, or microbes, spoiled the juice. He carried out similar studies with milk and wine.

The next problem was to discover how microbes got into the juice. More experiments made it clear to Pasteur that microbes float free in the air. They can *contaminate* any liquid exposed to the air, even for a short time. Pasteur also discovered that by gently heating a contaminated liquid the microbes could be destroyed without damaging the taste of the liquid. This process is called pasteurization. Today fresh milk is treated like this to ensure it contains no harmful microbes.

Pasteur's ideas were not immediately understood by other chemists. The medical profession was interested but unconvinced. Eventually, because Pasteur's scientific work had been so careful and because he was very good at presenting his ideas in public, his theories were accepted and became the basis for a great deal of research.

Pasteur also started to do medical research. He wanted to see if special microbes caused disease. He did not manage to identify individual germs because microscopes were not yet powerful enough to see anything so small. A German doctor, Robert Koch, also worked on this important problem. He invented a new way of preparing the samples to be studied under the microscope. And, in 1878, had the great triumph of identifying the first disease germs to be observed by man. They were germs of the disease called anthrax.

During his research Pasteur became interested in why a mild case of a serious

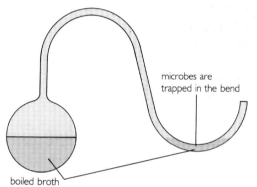

microbes are trapped in the bend

boiled broth

disease or a closely related illness seemed to give protection against a deadly attack of the disease. He carried out a long and successful investigation into the mysteries of *vaccination*, continuing the work of an English doctor, Edward Jenner.

A cure for smallpox

In 1796, Jenner had observed that dairy maids frequently caught a mild *rash* called cowpox from the cows they milked. But they never caught the terrible disease, smallpox. Smallpox killed thousands upon thousands of people in Europe at that time, and anyone who recovered from it was usually left pitted with scars. It was also one of the most dreadful diseases in Africa and the Far East. In some places tribes had special gods to whom they sacrificed, hoping they would keep smallpox away.

After studying the symptoms of both

◄Louis Pasteur (1822–95) did his work in laboratories that looked very different from modern ones. His equipment was very simple and the success or failure of research depended on the care and precision of the person making the observation.

◄This oddly shaped glass bottle was an essential part of the experiment Pasteur devised which proved that microbes did not suddenly come to life in something dead. He filled the globe with broth that had been boiled to kill all microbes. Because air could reach the broth only through the bent tube new microbes were trapped in the fluid in the bend and could not reach the broth. It stayed fresh. When the bottle and tube were shaken violently, air and the trapping fluid got through to the broth and the microbes caused it to go bad.

the mild disease and the killer it so resembled, Jenner guessed that the mild disease stimulated the body in some way so that it could fight off successfully any attack from smallpox. To prove his idea he carried out a very daring experiment. He infected a young boy with cowpox by scraping his skin with a needle contaminated by the disease. The boy got cowpox and quickly recovered. Later, when he was perfectly healthy, Jenner repeated the process but used a needle contaminated by smallpox. The boy remained in perfect health. Jenner had carried out the first vaccination. This type of health protection is called vaccination after 'vacca', the Latin word for cow.

Although Jenner did not understand how vaccination worked, his technique was so successful it is now used to protect us not only from smallpox but from many other serious diseases. Vaccination for smallpox was accepted quickly, partly because people were so terrified of the disease and the scars it left and partly because Jenner's treatment won the support of some wealthy and aristocratic ladies, willing to try anything which offered hope of escaping smallpox.

A new treatment for disease

After studying Jenner's techniques, Pasteur was able to devise several important new vaccines. He produced two for animal diseases, anthrax and chicken cholera, but his most famous one was for rabies, a disease which, if untreated, is almost always fatal. It is caused by the bite of an infected warm-blooded animal, usually a dog. Pasteur's vaccine could be given to a person even after they had been bitten, provided they were brought to a doctor quickly enough. His vaccine has saved thousands from a horrible death.

▶ This cartoon shows what people feared would happen when vaccination against smallpox was introduced. Fortunately the cartoonist was wrong and vaccination soon became a valuable weapon in the fight against disease. The baby (**top right**) does not even realize that the nice-tasting syrup he is being given is not a treat, but actually a vaccine to protect him against polio – a disease that can cripple its victims.

The Cow Pock — or — the Wonderful Effects of the New Inoculation! — Vide the Publications of ye Anti Vaccine Society.

WARFARE IN THE BODY – HOW IMMUNITY WORKS

The discoveries of Jenner and Pasteur began to show how the body defends itself against disease and how medicine can make this defence more effective. The body rejects or destroys harmful substances that enter it by what is called the 'immune response'. As Pasteur discovered, the air is full of tiny organisms, some of which are very harmful. Our body has several natural barriers to prevent these microbes entering. The moisture in our mouth and nose catches and filters out some. It also contains a chemical that can kill many others. Microbes passing from the mouth to the stomach are destroyed there by the powerful stomach *acids*. These acids are so strong that sometimes they destroy something which could help us. This is why some medicines must be injected directly into the blood rather than swallowed in pills or a liquid. Our skin, too, protects us. When we cut ourselves

bacteria and viruses have a chance to enter our body. Even a small cut must always be carefully cleansed and protected until new skin grows.

Harmful bacteria and viruses cause disease because they upset the ordinary way our body *cells* work. Bacteria are small living things and they feed on substances within us. They grow rapidly, multiply and travel through the blood to disturb many parts of the body. Different sorts of harmful bacteria attack different cells. Some may attack nerve cells, others lung cells, others may attack our *glands* or stomach. Viruses, which are very much smaller than bacteria and therefore much more difficult to see even under powerful microscopes, are not living things in the same way bacteria are. They are tiny protein packages. Once within the body they, too, multiply and destroy healthy tissue. Many of the most serious diseases known to medicine are caused by viruses.

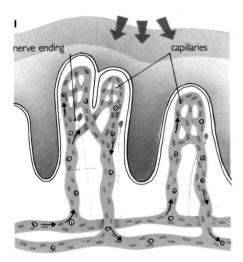

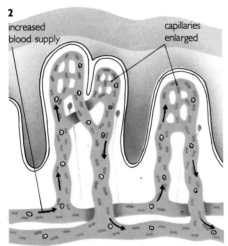

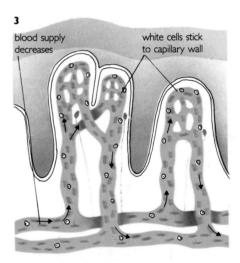

▲ This is what happens when any part of our body becomes *inflamed*. **1** A section through the skin highly magnified. Red arrows show injury at the skin surface (brown).
2 Chemicals from injured skin cells make the capillaries enlarge and more blood flows

in them causing redness of the skin.
3 White blood cells move to the capillary walls and with some blood fluid leak out, swelling the skin tissue.
4 Healing starts. Inflammation can occur from an injury or cut but it also can occur within the body when some part is attacked

by viruses or bacteria. The capillaries are the tiniest blood vessels in the body and many are visible only under a microscope. All diseases with names ending in 'itis' are inflammations. The best known is appendicitis, inflammation of the appendix.

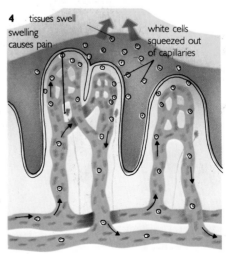

◀Plants, too, have natural immunity. Two of the buds on this apple tree are healthy, while the other two have been attacked by powdery mildew.

An illness caused by a virus or bacteria may give us a pain, perhaps in our head, stomach, throat, arms or legs. Pain is a signal that something in our body is not working as it should.

Natural defences against disease
From the moment we are born, we have cells within us that can destroy harmful substances. They are called phagocytes from the Greek term meaning 'cell-eaters'. They are special white blood cells that literally eat up harmful bacteria. Sometimes we can see them at work. If a cut becomes infected the skin around it gets *inflamed*, that is hot, red and swollen. If the infection is bad, a nasty yellowish substance called pus is formed. All this shows that the phagocytes are doing their job. Blood vessels around the cut become enlarged, rushing extra phagocytes to the place where the bacteria entered. Pus is formed by the bodies of thousands upon thousands of

◀A blood sample seen through a low-powered microscope. The sample has been stained to make the cells show up better. The large cell with purple patches is a white cell and the rest are red cells.

▶These two cells are macrophages, part of the body's defence against disease. The one in the front of the photograph is about to surround a small round particle that might cause the body harm.

phagocytes that have killed and digested the bacteria.

The body has another natural weapon, active acquired *immunity*. This is how vaccination works. When any harmful protein, whether it is from a *bacterium*, a virus or even a pollen grain from a plant, enters the body, the blood begins to manufacture an opposing protein called an *antibody*. Antibodies are made by specialized white blood cells. The antibody destroys the invader. If the blood manufactures the antibody very quickly, the disease germs are destroyed so fast that we have virtually no symptoms. Once the body has manufactured antibodies against a certain harmful protein it remembers this and the next time it is invaded by that protein it manufactures large quantities of the right antibody much more quickly.

We now understand that vaccination is a way of teaching the body how to manufacture antibodies quickly to fight against serious disease germs. Each vaccine, however, can work only for one type of germ. Some are made from the germs themselves, specially treated so they are weak and no longer dangerous. Others are made from dead bacteria or viruses. Some are special varieties of the germ. For some diseases, doctors give patients antibodies already made in someone else's blood, or even in the blood of an animal. This is called 'passive' immunity and lasts for only a short time. Much medical research since Pasteur's day has been aimed at discovering which bacterium or virus is responsible for which disease. When this is known, researchers seek a way to encourage the body to make the right immune response.

▼ The condition of some patients, particularly babies, is so poor that even the specially purified air of the operating rooms is not pure enough. To reduce the risk of infection even more, the patient is enclosed in a transparent bubble full of germ-free air. There are specially shaped plastic 'arms' and 'hands' into which the surgeons and nurses fit their own arms and hands, so that they never actually touch the patient with their own hands.

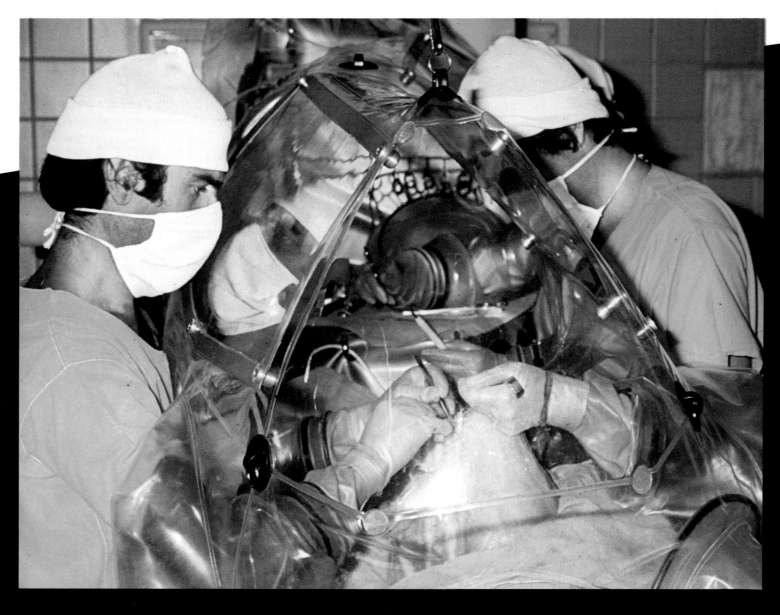

3

FIGHTING AGAINST DISEASE

WARFARE AGAINST GERMS – CLEANLINESS AND ANTISEPTICS

▲ Compare these two photographs with others in this book to see how knowledge of the dangers of germs changed the way doctors operate.
Above The operating room of St Thomas's Hospital, London, built in 1821 and used for 40 years. It was actually in the loft of St Thomas's Church.
Right To use this early anesthetic equipment the patient had the mask placed over the face and inhaled chloroform from sponges soaked in it.

When doctors and scientists began to appreciate the link between germs and disease, medicine was able to make more rapid progress. Another important link, between dirt and disease, began to be understood at about the same time. In the early nineteenth century, people who had

a simple injury such as a cut arm or leg, often died of gangrene. This is a terrible disease in which the flesh begins to rot while someone is still alive. Women having babies were frightened of puerperal fever, an *infection* which killed many soon after they had given birth. For many diseases there was little hope and huge numbers of people died, even when given the best medical care then available. Doctors at that time gave little thought to cleanliness in hospitals or when looking after their patients.

A revolutionary idea

One of the first signs of change came in Hungary. Ignaz Semmelweis gradually became convinced that doctors themselves were spreading puerperal fever from one woman to another because they did not wash their hands between examining patients or after inspecting the body of someone who had died of the disease. Semmelweis made doctors and students wash their hands carefully and in his hospital the death rate from puerperal fever dropped dramatically. But because Pasteur's work on germs had not yet been done, most of Semmelweis's colleagues laughed at his ideas and few copied his good practices.

The discovery of antiseptics

In Scotland, Joseph Lister read Pasteur's work on microbes in 1865. He then made the kind of inspired medical guess that Jenner had made about vaccination, nearly a century earlier. He became convinced that microbes were responsible

22

for gangrene and he determined to find a way to kill them. First he devised a new way to clean wounds. He gently washed them with a clean cloth dipped in a mild solution of carbolic acid. Before Lister tried this treatment in one hospital, more than 45% of patients who had lost an arm or leg died of gangrene. After beginning the carbolic treatment, only 15% died. Like Semmelweis, Lister found that his ideas were often attacked and ridiculed. As the work of Pasteur, and later Robert Koch, became better known and because his own medical successes were so great, Lister's methods gradually were adopted in more and more hospitals. Doctors accepted the use of *antiseptics*, the name for substances which act against sepsis or infection.

Lister continued throughout his life to find new ways to improve the use of antiseptics. He invented a spray to attack microbes in the air. He demanded that the places in hospitals where wounds were treated or operations performed be kept as clean as possible.

Cleanliness and the use of substances like soap, alcohol or carbolic acid helped reduce deaths from many diseases. But the cells in our body are very delicate, so strong antiseptic chemicals can only be used outside the body. Many antiseptics can burn or damage the skin. Unfortunately, antiseptics can kill only bacteria so the viruses that cause many diseases escape. Some varieties of bacteria protect themselves by forming a hard outer case called a spore and these also escape antiseptics.

Finally, in the 1890s, Robert Koch made yet another great contribution to medicine. He discovered that hot steam killed all germs. This meant that doctors could operate with instruments that were sterilized, in other words really germ free. Even bandages could be treated in this way. But germs can lurk in the folds of even the cleanest skin, and this is too delicate to be exposed to hot steam, so doctors began to wear sterilized rubber gloves for operations and some examinations. Although the battle was not over, germs were losing on many battlegrounds.

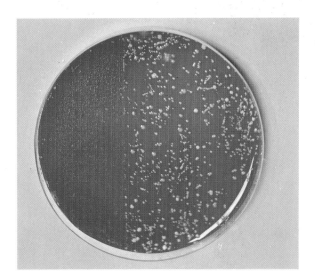

◄A fly has walked across this plate. But before that the left-hand side of the plate was treated with antiseptic. You can see that the germs from the fly's feet have been able to flourish on the untreated, right-hand side of the plate but, on the left, they have been killed by the antiseptic.

MAGIC BULLETS AND WONDER DRUGS

As well as trying to discover what causes certain diseases and how to prevent people from getting them, doctors and other scientists spend a great deal of time and effort trying to find ways of curing people once they have become ill. Giving something to stimulate the body's own immune response is often not possible because too many bacteria or viruses may be there already. The patient must be given something that will destroy them quickly. Whatever is given must be powerful enough to kill the bacteria, but must not harm the body. This is why doctors cannot inject antiseptic into us when we have a bacterial disease. The antiseptic would certainly kill the bacteria, but it would act as a poison and kill us too!

For centuries the only effective drugs were made from plants or the bark of trees. These often contain substances that ease the symptoms of many diseases but they are not strong enough to act against serious infections. There is another problem, too. The helpful substance in the plant may be strong or weak depending on the ground where the plant grew, the weather and when it was picked. It was obvious that remedies from plants alone were not enough.

In the 1900s, a German scientist, Paul Ehrlich, began a systematic search for a chemical 'magic bullet', a substance which, when injected into the body, would seek out harmful bacteria and kill only them. Much of his work was based on the

► Under a microscope, aspirin, one of the most common modern drugs, looks like this. It is made from the chemical salicylic acid. We are often given it to help a headache, toothache, fever or pains in muscles and joints.

► Both chemical and antibiotic drugs are often taken in capsules. These small containers hold a carefully measured amount of a drug. They are tasteless and easy to swallow. Once in the stomach, the little container dissolves, releasing the drug so it can be absorbed like food.

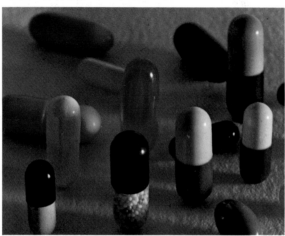

experiments of his fellow countryman, Robert Koch. Koch had noticed that certain chemical dyes were attracted to certain groups of bacteria. That curious action helped Koch identify the germs that caused several serious diseases, especially tuberculosis. Ehrlich continued along Koch's path. He carried out test after test on different groups of bacteria and different chemicals. On the six hundred and sixth attempt, he found his magic bullet, a drug he named Salvarsan. It was a chemical that attacked and killed the organisms that caused the disease known as syphilis. This disease caused blindness, madness, paralysis and agonizing death and at that time there was no cure. Salvarsan was the first drug that came from a group of chemicals called sulphonamides. Many years later, during World War 2, new drugs from the same family of chemicals saved the lives of many injured soldiers.

Penicillin – the first antibiotic
Doctors also searched for helpful drugs among the micro-organisms themselves. They noticed that some attacked others or prevented them from growing. These micro-organisms are called *antibiotics*. The first attempts to make useful drugs

from antibiotics were not successful because they usually did more harm than good. In 1928, an English doctor, Alexander Fleming, was studying a bacterium that was responsible for many serious infections. He had *colonies* of the bacteria growing on several laboratory dishes. One day he saw that a dish was contaminated with mold. On that dish the deadly bacteria had stopped growing. The mold was called *penicillium notatum*. From it, Fleming made penicillin, the first and still one of the safest and most effective of the large 'family' of antibiotics. Because antibiotic drugs act so quickly and cures are so dramatic, people nicknamed them 'wonder drugs'.

WEAPONS AGAINST PAIN

Trying to stop pain is an important task for medical science. We all can experience different amounts of pain from very little to very severe. Very great pain can make a person unconscious. Pain can be sharp and sudden or it may go on and on, like an aching tooth. It may seem to move about the body or stay in one place. Sometimes when a person loses an arm or leg, the limb that is not there still feels painful because the torn ends of the nerves are still sending pain signals to the brain. Doctors always listen carefully to the way a patient describes pain because this is an important clue for correct diagnosis.

It is difficult to measure pain. Scientists know that each person has a different 'pain threshold'. Your pain threshold is the point beyond which pain becomes difficult to bear. For a person with a low pain threshold even a quick injection may be very painful. A person with a high pain threshold can receive a bad wound yet still be able to cope with the pain. No one understands why there is this difference. The most likely explanation is that each person's brain understands its own body's pain messages in a slightly different way and at a different speed. The sensation of pain travels to the brain along thousands and thousands of nerve cells throughout the body.

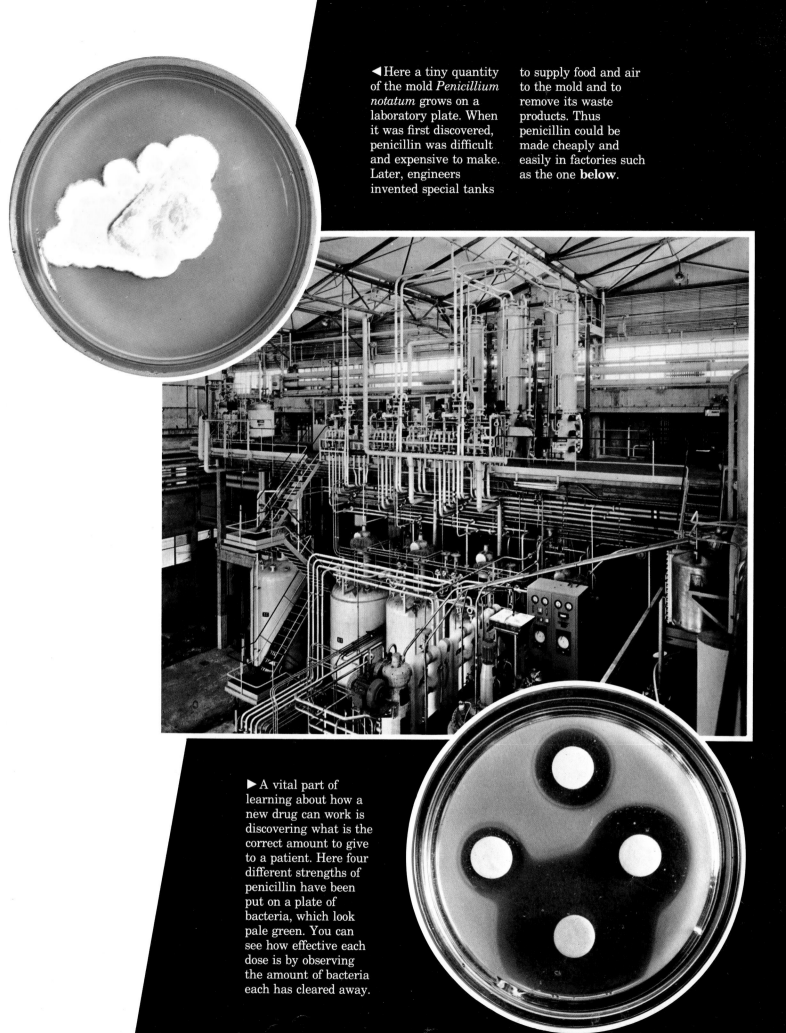

◀ Here a tiny quantity of the mold *Penicillium notatum* grows on a laboratory plate. When it was first discovered, penicillin was difficult and expensive to make. Later, engineers invented special tanks to supply food and air to the mold and to remove its waste products. Thus penicillin could be made cheaply and easily in factories such as the one **below**.

▶ A vital part of learning about how a new drug can work is discovering what is the correct amount to give to a patient. Here four different strengths of penicillin have been put on a plate of bacteria, which look pale green. You can see how effective each dose is by observing the amount of bacteria each has cleared away.

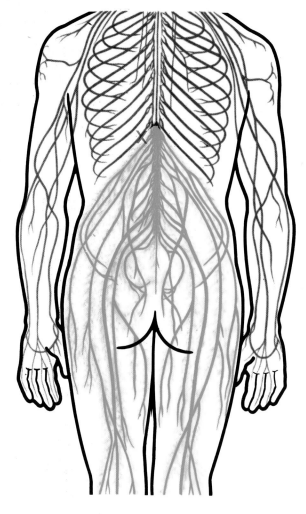

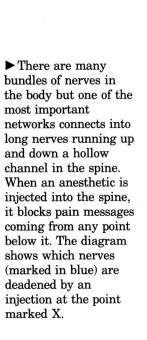

►There are many bundles of nerves in the body but one of the most important networks connects into long nerves running up and down a hollow channel in the spine. When an anesthetic is injected into the spine, it blocks pain messages coming from any point below it. The diagram shows which nerves (marked in blue) are deadened by an injection at the point marked X.

To control pain, doctors try to find safe ways to slow down or block these messages. This search has been going on for thousands of years, long before anyone knew how the nerves and brain were connected. Alcohol in wine and spirits slows down and muddles the brain. For centuries people were given large quantities to drink before an operation. Many ancient herbal remedies were mixed with wine to dull pain. Opium, a drug made from the poppy, *papaver somniferum*, has also been used since ancient times to cause drowsiness and sleep. It, too, was used as a pain killer. Neither opium nor alcohol were perfect pain killers and each often did patients much more harm than good.

The real 'laughing gas'
In the 1800s, Humphry Davy, an English chemist, discovered that breathing in a gas took away the pain of toothache and made him feel happy. The gas, nitrous oxide, was nicknamed 'laughing gas'. It is a true *anesthetic* – a substance that takes away the power of feeling and, in large quantities, can make a person *unconscious*. Soon after Davy's discovery,

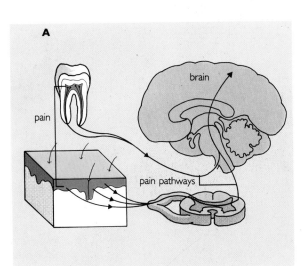

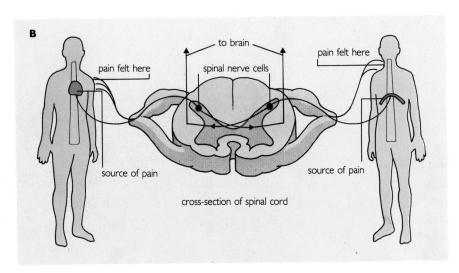

▲These diagrams show some of the pathways pain takes in the body. **A** shows how a toothache or a painful blow to the skin sends its message to the brain. The pain from the tooth goes directly into the brain. The pain from the skin travels a longer route via the spine to the brain. **B** shows how pain can sometimes be 'referred' to another part of the body. The man on the left has a heart condition, but feels the pain, not in his heart but in his left shoulder. The man on the right feels the pain in his neck and shoulders, although the source of the pain is actually in his abdomen.

another scientist, Michael Faraday, found that breathing ether also stopped feelings of pain and made a patient unconscious. Doctors were cautious about using ether or nitrous oxide because they were worried about the possible after-effects on their patients. At first it was very difficult to judge how much to give someone but equipment was invented that made administration safe and easy. The first operation using anesthetics was performed in Boston, Massachusetts, in 1846.

The Queen approved

After that, discoveries followed rapidly. Chloroform, an anesthetic that made *childbirth* less painful, was discovered and tested by a Scottish doctor, James Young Simpson. Queen Victoria was given it for the birth of one of her children and found it excellent. Immediately its use was welcomed by doctors and patients everywhere. Cocaine, a powerful drug obtained from the coca leaves, was developed. It is used to give partial or local anesthesia, that is a blocking of pain in just one part of the body without making the patient unconscious. The anesthetics used by dentists today are often of this type.

Because anesthetics have such a powerful effect on the brain and body, doctors always have special extra training in how to use them. Many anesthetics affect a person's breathing and blood pressure temporarily, and so breathing may have to be kept going by a machine (respirator). So patients must be watched carefully as long as the drug is acting in the body. *Analgesics*, drugs that lessen pain without affecting a person's ability to think and feel, are now receiving a great deal of attention. They are needed for people who suffer long-term painful diseases such as *arthritis*, rheumatism, nerve pain, or cancer.

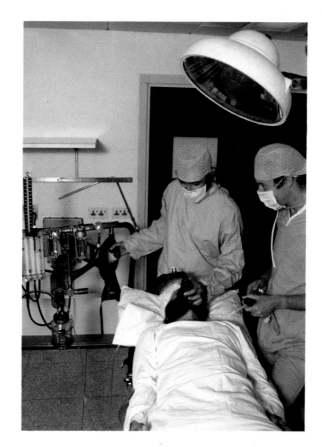

◄The specialist who administers anesthetics during an operation is called an anesthetist. Here one is checking his equipment. The gas cylinders contain nitrous oxide and oxygen to help the patient's breathing. The dials and instruments help the anesthetist measure the flow of gases exactly. The mask in his right hand will cover the patient's face.

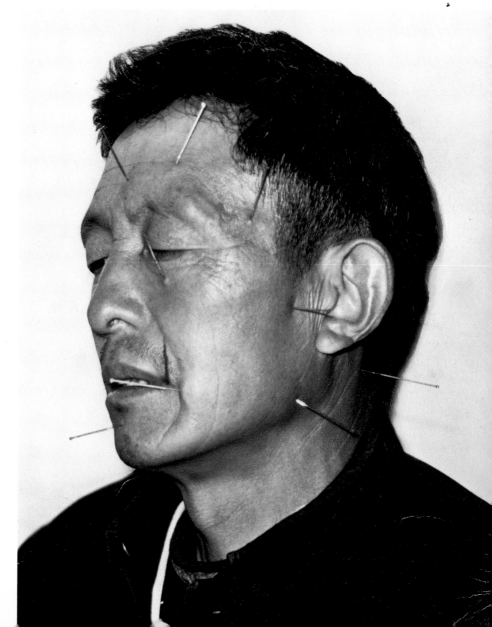

► This man has acupuncture needles inserted all over his face. Acupuncture is an ancient Chinese method of medical treatment that has been used instead of anesthetics in some operations. Although no-one knows how it works, it has been practiced in China for many centuries.

CONTROLLING THREE KILLERS

We can appreciate the hard work of many doctors and scientists since the 1850s when we know that medicine today can control tuberculosis, pneumonia and typhoid. These three diseases are caused by bacteria and a hundred years ago killed tens of thousands of people each year. Another type of pneumonia is caused by a virus and it, too, can now be cured.

Tuberculosis

Tuberculosis and pneumonia attack the lungs. When we breathe in, oxygen, a gas that is essential for life, is transferred from the air into the blood in the thousands of tiny air sacs (called alveoli) that make up our lungs. When the lungs cannot work properly because of infection, we die. Typhoid attacks the intestine, the long tube below the stomach where food continues to be digested and absorbed into the body after leaving the stomach. If this process is disrupted seriously the person dies quickly and in great pain.

Tuberculosis bacteria settle in the lungs and when the conditions are favourable become active and multiply. They feed on the lung tissue and cause little lumps to form. This irritation makes a sufferer cough. Tiny droplets of moisture from the cough contain more bacteria and thus the disease is easily passed from one person to another. Today antibiotics can destroy the TB bacteria and if a lung is too damaged by the disease, part of it can be removed quite safely. There is an effective vaccination against tuberculosis as well. In countries where people have a poor diet and live in crowded, unhealthy conditions, governments often organize huge vaccination campaigns. Mass X-ray screening is also used to detect the disease in an early, easily curable stage. Cows, too, are tested for tuberculosis because scientists have discovered that cows' milk can contain the harmful bacteria.

Pneumonia

The bacteria that cause pneumonia are called pneumococci. They are very interesting because there are always some in our mouth and throat. Usually there are very few of them and they do not make us ill. But if we become run down, perhaps because we have had some other illness and have lost our appetite for good, nourishing food, the pneumococci can suddenly begin to multiply. Large

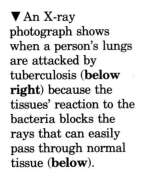
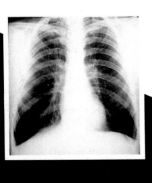

▼ An X-ray photograph shows when a person's lungs are attacked by tuberculosis (**below right**) because the tissues' reaction to the bacteria blocks the rays that can easily pass through normal tissue (**below**).

▼ When treating pneumonia, as with tuberculosis, X-rays help the doctor to see what is happening inside a patient's lungs. On the right is a normal lung, fully expanded within the rib cage. Pneumonia has struck the lung on the left.

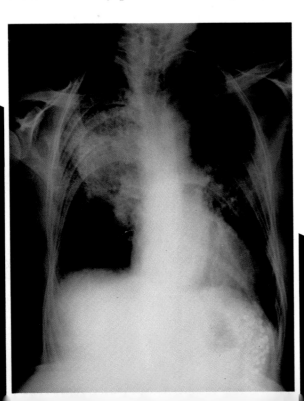
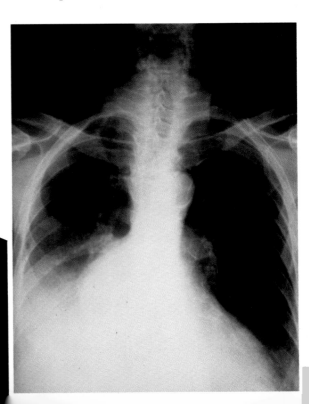

numbers go down into the lungs and there they cause the lungs to fill up with liquid. Breathing becomes very shallow, rapid and painful. The victim runs a very high temperature, has a terrible headache and pains in the chest and shoulders. Fortunately antibiotics are very effective at killing these bacteria. If they are given quickly, a patient's fever will disappear and he or she will recover rapidly.

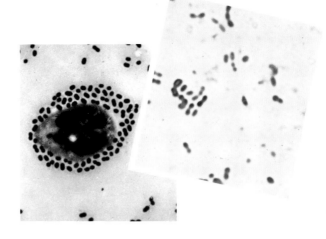

◀ The bacteria that cause pneumonia often form pairs (**far left**) or start chains (**left**). This is how they look under the microscope.

Typhoid

The bacteria that cause typhoid live in dirty food and water. They are easily carried from place to place by flies. Before scientists understood this, serious outbreaks of typhoid called *epidemics* regularly killed millions of people, especially in crowded cities during hot weather. Now modern rules about cleanliness in food preparation in restaurants and factories, as well as proper public water supplies and sewage systems, save people from this disease. Typhoid is particularly dangerous because it can also be spread by carriers. These are people who carry the disease in their bodies, but do not become ill with it. They can however, spread the disease to others. The bacteria are excreted from the body when someone with the disease goes to the toilet, so if a carrier does not wash his hands the bacteria can easily pass into food or water and infect someone who is not immune.

In its early stages typhoid seems dangerously like a less deadly illness. A person becomes feverish, tired, and does not want to eat. Later a rash develops. When the bacteria begin to attack the intestines the disease has reached a critical stage and can be fatal. Typhoid is still common in parts of the world where the supply of drinking water is poor and there are no modern sewage systems. That is why people travelling to these places are advised to have typhoid injections. People are also vaccinated against typhoid whenever a disaster like an earthquake or flood disrupts the water supply. Sewage can escape from broken pipes and contaminate the water and food thus quickly spreading the disease.

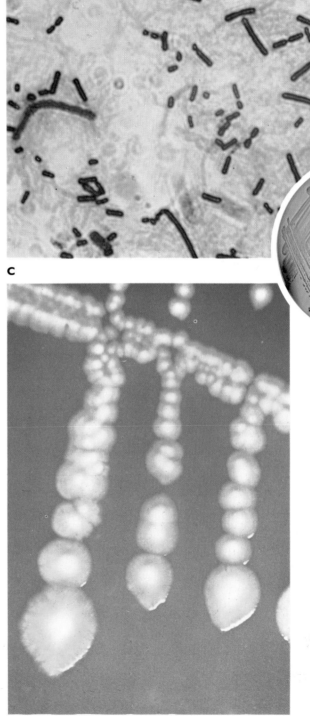

▲ Groups of typhoid bacteria form colonies or large clumps as they grow on the jelly that feeds them on a laboratory plate.
A A tiny sample of excrement from someone suspected of having typhoid is put on the plate. In the sample the single bacteria are too small to be seen without a microscope. They quickly form large colonies which are easily seen. **B** Under the microscope chains of rod-shaped typhoid bacteria are easy to identify. **C** This is a close-up of a laboratory sample of colonies of typhoid bacteria.

VIRUSES, MYSTERIOUS ENEMIES

Many diseases that attack people, plants and animals are caused not by bacteria but by mysterious things called viruses. Viruses are so tiny that even when they have multiplied millions of times they do not form visible colonies. They cannot survive on jelly in a laboratory. They always need living cells. Scientists had to discover ways to keep groups of cells alive, *tissue* cultures, before they were able to study viruses closely. Many familiar diseases are caused by viruses: the common cold, measles, mumps, influenza, smallpox and polio. You do not have to be near someone who has had a virus disease to catch it, because many viruses can survive a long time away from their most recent host. The virus that causes 'flu can infect someone who breathes in dust nearly two weeks after a previous sufferer has coughed or sneezed into it.

One of the oddest things about viruses is that scientists are not sure if they ought to say they are alive or not. They are not living the way bacteria are. They do not feed on anything. They cannot move about by themselves. They do not reproduce in any usual way. They just invade healthy cells and those cells then begin to make more viruses.

Studying viruses and the diseases they cause is difficult because viruses react in strange ways and because they are so small. Now that scientists have electron microscopes, microscopes that work by bombarding a sample of material with electrons instead of ordinary light, viruses can be observed. As 20,000 viruses can fit comfortably inside one bacterium, and one bacterium is invisible except under a good light microscope, you can understand how small viruses are.

All viruses are made up of two substances, protein and nucleic acid. Protein is the basic building block of all living cells. Nucleic acid is a substance that seems to instruct cells to produce a certain type of protein. In other words, nucleic acid is a kind of messenger that tells cells in our bodies or in plants and animals to build what the body needs. When a virus enters a normal cell, its nucleic acid takes over and the cells begin to produce viruses.

The body's defences

We now know that there are two defences against viruses. One is the same as the defence against bacteria. The body produces antibodies in the blood. This takes time and a different sort of antibody is needed for each type of virus. Once the body learns to produce the antibody, it will be immune against another attack, at least for a time. However, virus diseases, like the common cold and influenza,

▼ A fertile hen's egg is injected with a virus (**right**) and the viruses multiply rapidly inside the tissue of the embryo chick (**below**). This is the way many viruses are grown in laboratories before they are turned into vaccines.

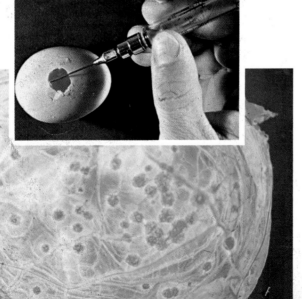

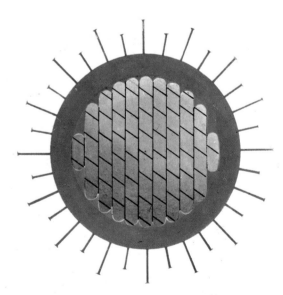

▲ An influenza virus looks like this. It has an outer wall of fat and protein and inside the protein units are stacked like bricks. The rods stick to red cells in the blood and force them to clump together. There are three main types of 'flu virus but each one type has many subdivisions or strains.

cannot easily be defeated by vaccination. These familiar diseases have many different sorts of virus. Each needs a unique antibody that takes time to produce.

Scientists have recently discovered that the body has another way of fighting viruses. As soon as a virus enters a healthy cell, the cell begins to produce a substance called interferon. Unlike an antibody in the blood that can fight against only one type of virus, interferon can fight against all viruses. It stops them multiplying. It jams their messages, so to

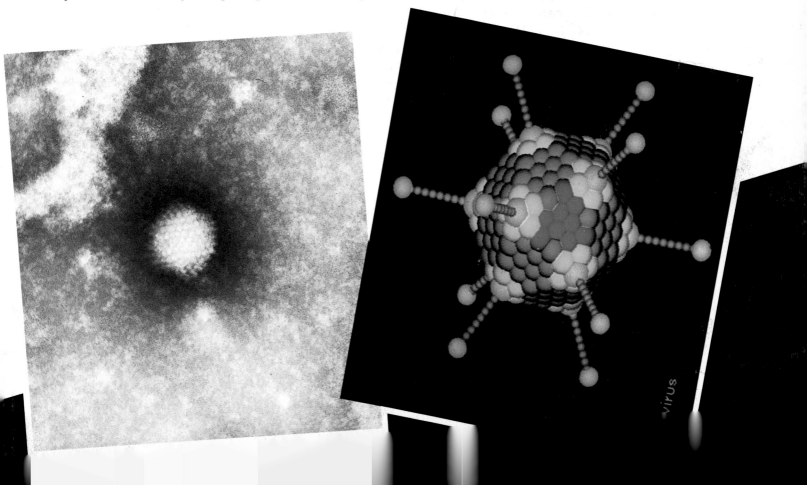

virus

speak. Now doctors and scientists are trying to discover how they can encourage cells to make interferon quickly when under attack or how interferon can be made outside the body and given to people who are ill. As yet, there is no easy way of producing this substance. It may be a long time before it can be used against viruses the way penicillin is used against bacteria. Everyone is watching this research very closely because some forms of cancer are probably caused by viruses. Eventually interferon may be a powerful weapon against one of the most dreaded diseases in the world today.

PARASITES

Viruses and bacteria are not the only threats to our health. There are many tiny insects, animals and some fungi, plants that belong to the same family as mushrooms, that can live on us and in us and cause disease. These are called *parasites*. Most have very complicated lives. They may be born in water or in the body of another insect or animal before moving on to infect a human being. When they settle on or in a person they gradually weaken the body, destroying its defences against the disease.

Typhus
Fleas and lice are well-known parasites. These insects live on human beings as well as animals and take food from their blood. They also carry with them viruses and bacteria that cause other diseases. Rickettsiae are tiny creatures that look like miniature lobsters under a microscope. They often start life living in insects such as fleas and lice. When they pass on to a human being through the bite of a louse, they cause typhus. This killer disease has a Greek name that means cloudy or hazy. Typhus begins with terrible headaches that confuse the mind. Then the sufferer develops a dark red rash, a high fever alternating with chills and eventually blood escapes from damaged vessels in the brain or heart.

▼ These are three different types of virus that cause illness in humans. **Below** One of the many types of 'flu virus. **Below right** The virus of *Herpes simplex* that causes cold sores. **Bottom** Pox viruses always cause infections with rashes.

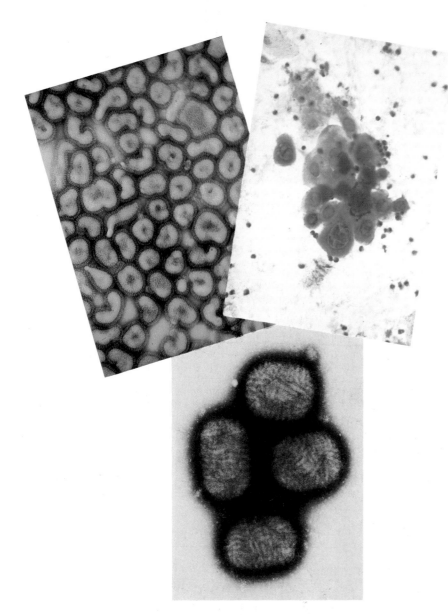

▶ A bed bug is a parasite. At night it emerges from dirty bedding and feeds on human blood. This picture shows a bed bug enlarged many times. Actually it is about a centimeter long and a third of a centimeter wide.

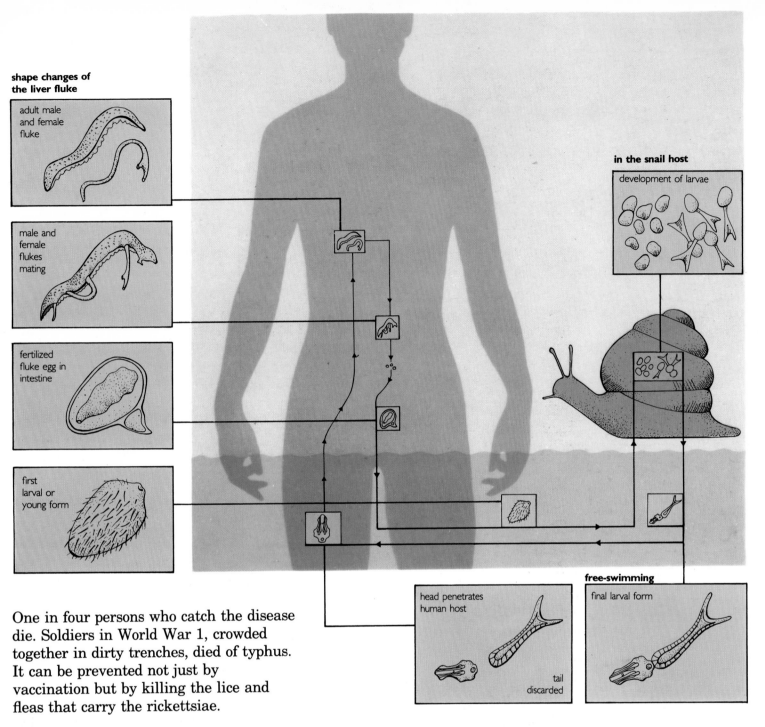

shape changes of the liver fluke

adult male and female fluke

male and female flukes mating

fertilized fluke egg in intestine

first larval or young form

in the snail host

development of larvae

head penetrates human host

tail discarded

free-swimming

final larval form

One in four persons who catch the disease die. Soldiers in World War 1, crowded together in dirty trenches, died of typhus. It can be prevented not just by vaccination but by killing the lice and fleas that carry the rickettsiae.

Parasitic worms

Several different sorts of worm are parasites. Flukes are flat and leaf shaped. Roundworms look like shiny white earthworms. Tapeworms are long and flat and can grow to enormous lengths of several feet inside a person. One parasite, an amoeba, causes amoebic dysentery, a disease of the intestines that is very common in hot countries. Unlike the flukes and most worm parasites, it can pass directly from one human being to another.

Diseases caused by fungi usually spread very quickly either by direct touch or if someone who is well touches an object that has already been contaminated with the disease. Like mushrooms, fungi have

▲ A parasitic worm, the liver fluke, causes disease in sheep and human beings. Each adult fluke can produce 20,000 eggs a day. They pass down into the host's intestines and out with waste matter. The eggs change into larvae, the young form of the fluke. They find a temporary home in snails. Inside the snail, the young fluke begins to change its shape. It leaves the snail, loses its tail and makes a hard coat. It then attaches itself to watercress or other plants that grow in or near water. If a sheep or human being eats these plants the young fluke will pass into the body, grow up, mate and produce thousands more eggs while living off and damaging the liver of its host.

spores, tiny little seed-like things that grow into new fungi. These float easily in the air and can survive a long time on unclean surfaces, especially if they are warm and damp. Athlete's foot is a painful skin disease caused by fungi, and thrush, a very common uncomfortable complaint of the mouth, is too.

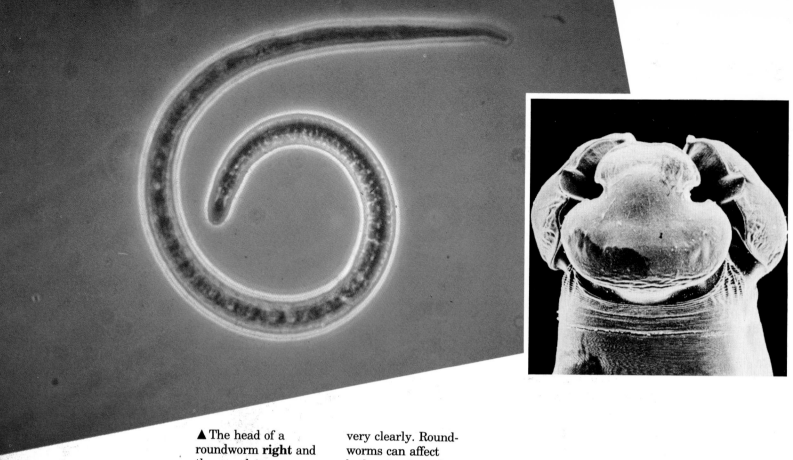

▲ The head of a roundworm **right** and the complete worm **above**. The head has been magnified 125 times and the worm's three thick lips show very clearly. Roundworms can affect both animals and humans. We may get these worms if we eat undercooked pork.

Malaria

In hot, damp, tropical parts of the world, malaria is a disease that causes much suffering and death. A special type of mosquito that lives in swamps carries inside itself even smaller creatures, plasmodia. These are the parasites that cause malaria. Once they get into a person's blood through a mosquito bite, they settle into the red blood cells. There they divide to make many smaller parasites. When a healthy blood cell is totally taken over by the parasites, they burst out and move into fresh cells. As this happens, the victim suffers from terrible chills and fever. Malaria is a difficult disease to cure. To prevent it, governments and international organizations work to spray with poison and drain the swamps where the mosquito that carries the parasites live. Sleeping sickness (Trypanosoma), a disease that weakens and kills cattle and people in many parts of Africa and South America, is also carried by a parasite. It is carried from one *host* to another by flies.

▲ Malaria still causes more deaths than any other disease in the world. As swamps are drained and new drugs, or combinations of drugs, are discovered, this death rate is dropping and some places are now free of the disease for the first time.

STARTING OUT WITH PROBLEMS

Two groups of problems do not, as a rule, have anything directly to do with viruses, bacteria or any other invader that upset the healthy working of our body. These illnesses are with a person from birth. They are usually called *congenital* illnesses. Some are also hereditary. That means a person has an illness or handicap because a parent, grand-parent or other ancestor also had it. It was passed on because the cells in the parent's body actually instructed the cells in the child's body to develop in some irregular way.

Genes and chromosomes

Within our cells are tiny particles called genes. These are organized in strings called chromosomes. When a cell from a mother's body combines with a cell from the father, half the chromosomes in the new cell that will grow into a baby come from the father and half from the mother. The chromosomes in the genes carry instructions for the development of all the parts of the new body, so a faulty chromosome will pass on faulty instructions. Epilepsy is an illness that appears to be caused by irregular patterns in the brain's work. An epileptic brain acts rather like an electric motor that sometimes sends out sparks and stops working for a few seconds. This can cause a person to suffer anything from an unexpected jerk of some muscles to a total collapse and loss of consciousness. A faulty gene could pass on this problem from parent to child.

Hemophilia is another hereditary illness. Only boys and men suffer the actual symptoms, but the faulty chromosomes that cause it are carried in the genes of girls and women. If a child has hemophilia, his blood will not clot properly. Even a slight scratch or cut will cause serious bleeding. A tiny bruise or bump can also cause bleeding inside the body and great pain.

Sometimes faulty chromosomes send on instructions that cause an organ to be formed in some way that is not quite perfect. A good example of this is an eye-ball that is too round or too flat, thus causing a person to be short- or long-

▲ Albinos are people, animals or plants that have no colour pigment in their skin. Somehow their genes made a mistake or lost an important piece of information. In a human being, albinism can cause health problems because the skin will not be able to protect itself from the harmful rays of the sun. Because there is no pigment in the eyes, they too can easily be damaged by strong light.

▶ This chart shows how one hereditary disease, hemophilia, can pass down through a family. Men have an X chromosome (red) and a Y (blue) chromosome. Women have two X chromosomes. If one of them is faulty (red and white) it can affect the way the blood clots. The women carry hemophilia. If a boy inherits a normal X from his mother, he will not have the disease (he has only one X chromosome). If he inherits a faulty X, he will. A girl will not because she is usually protected by the normal X from her father.

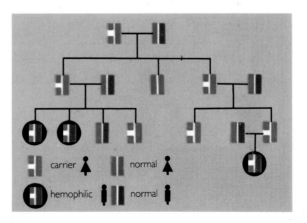

carrier ♀   normal ♀

hemophilic ♂   normal ♂

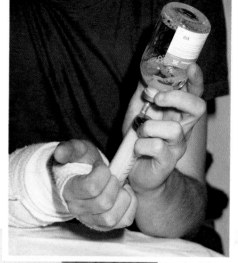

▼ Hemophilia, the illness in which the blood will not clot, can now be controlled successfully. The teenagers **below** are having their pulse rate monitored as the 'sleeves' expand and contract the blood vessels in their arm and leg after bleeding. Transfusions (**right**) to help the blood clot are now very simple.

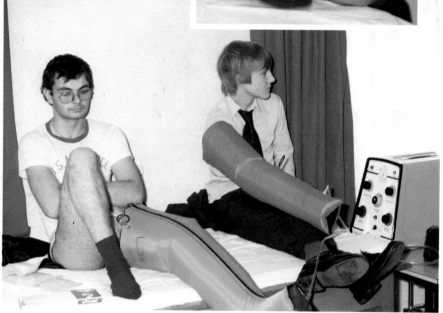

sighted. Fortunately this is a problem that is easily corrected with glasses or contact lenses.

Early problems
Sometimes the health problems of a new-born baby are not inherited but caused simply because its mother was ill or poorly fed while the baby was growing inside her. Sometimes the baby's own cells develop in some unusual way and some part of the body may not work properly after birth. Many babies are born with heart defects. Some of these are slight and disappear gradually as the baby grows. Others are very serious and years ago such a child, often called a 'blue baby' because the lack of oxygen in the blood made it appear quite blue, had little hope of a healthy, active life. Now doctors can operate on the heart and actually repair the damage. In many cases these babies can grow into healthy adults and later have no fear that their own children will suffer in any way. Now that doctors and scientists understand much more about how genes and chromosomes work and what causes congenital and hereditary diseases, they can give good advice to parents about the possible health problems of their children.

SNEEZES, RASHES AND UPSET TUMMIES

Smallpox, pneumonia, tuberculosis, malaria and heart disease can all cause death. Many other illnesses make us feel miserable and may reduce our enjoyment of life. Some children cannot have a puppy or kitten because being near a furry animal gives them a terrible rash or makes them sneeze and choke. Others cannot eat chocolate or drink milk because they will get a headache, stomach cramps or break out in small red spots. During the summer when grasses, plants and trees release into the air an almost invisible powder called pollen, millions of adults and children sneeze, cough and have painful, red eyes. They suffer from hayfever. All these problems are examples of *allergies*. If you have an allergy something that is perfectly harmless to most people, like milk, pollen grains or a

kitten's fur, affects your body in such a way that unpleasant symptoms occur.

The defence makes a mistake
As we know, the body's immune reaction fights off the invasion of harmful bacteria and viruses. But if this reaction goes wrong, it may act against some ordinary substance. When this happens, we call the substance an *antigen* or *allergy*. Antigens trigger the body into making antibodies in the blood in the same way as germs. If there are many antigens in the blood and they are not destroyed by antibodies, some get into the tissues, just like germs. Once in the tissues they irritate the cells. To protect themselves, the cells start to make a chemical called histamine. It is the histamine that produces the reactions like sneezes, coughs and rashes.

The easiest way to help someone with an allergy is to find out what is the allergen and then make sure the person avoids it. This is easy enough if the allergen comes from animal fur or a food like oysters or strawberries. It is impossible to do if the allergen is in pollen or ordinary household dust. Some people can be helped by injections of a pure allergen. Doctors gradually increase the dose as the body learns to cope with it. This is similar to the way a vaccine helps the body to fight against a disease. Scientists have also discovered drugs called antihistamines. They cancel out the effect of the histamines. But they cannot be given for every allergy, because they often have side-effects such as making the person who takes them drowsy and less alert.

Some unanswered questions

Doctors and scientists are doing a great deal of research about allergies. Many questions have to be answered. Why do some people have allergies from birth? Are they inherited? Why do some people acquire them later in life? Why do some allergies just disappear without treatment? What part does a patient's mind play in getting or curing an allergy? How can antihistamines be improved? There are no complete answers to any of these questions yet.

◄ This microscopic creature lives and breeds in household dust. It can cause symptoms of allergies such as coughs, rashes and sneezes in people.

▼ This honey bee is covered with yellow pollen from the flowers it has visited. Although pollen is a vital food for bees, some humans are allergic to it.

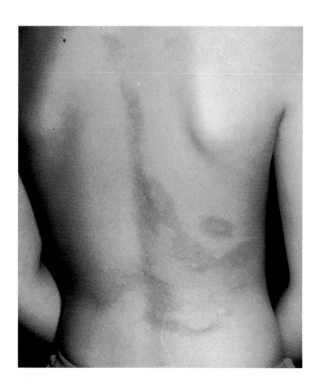

◄ This 10-year-old girl is suffering from very severe nettle rash.

► An allergy sufferer is being tested with many different substances to discover what triggers her allergy. The doctor inserts into the skin a tiny amount of substances that can cause allergies. If the skin becomes inflamed the doctor knows the patient is allergic to the substance. The white patches on the patient's back record what each one is.

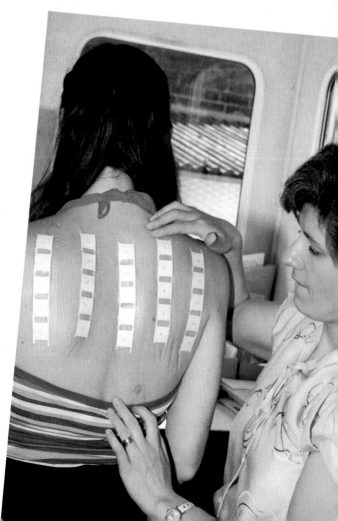

MIND AND BODY

▶ Sigmund Freud (left front) discovered that by getting the mentally disturbed to talk freely about their past, their fears, and their dreams, they could be helped to return to normal life. This became the basis of modern psychoanalysis. Carl Jung (right front), his pupil, expanded his ideas. He was particularly interested in the way a patient's dreams could reveal his relationship to himself, to others and to the culture in which he lived.

Allergies raise many questions that medicine still cannot answer. Mental illness, disorders and handicaps raise even more. We know that the brain, that large, wrinkled, organ in our skull is the most complicated and important part of our body. Sections of it organize the way we move, speak, hear, see, taste, touch and smell. Other sections constantly send and receive instructions to all the other organs of our body even as we sleep. The brain plays a part, although scientists do not fully understand how, in the way we feel about things, when we try to remember something, when we plan or when we dream. The brain is our thinking machine. It is the physical part of our mind.

If a baby's brain is injured, even before it is born, it may have a mental handicap throughout life. This means that its mind will not work in the same way as the minds of other children of the same age work. Sometimes a handicap will be very small. A child may just have a little trouble in speaking, moving or learning. Sometimes it may be severe, then the child will never be able to care for himself. He will need special help both in school and throughout life. Adults can become mentally handicapped through a severe injury, perhaps a car crash.

When people grow old, thousands of blood vessels in the brain may become clogged with material from the blood, in just the way old water pipes become blocked. The brain cells are starved of nourishment. When this happens people can develop mental problems and they become confused and forgetful.

Neuroses

Most mental illnesses, however, cannot easily be traced back to something going wrong in the physical working of the brain. There are two main types of mental illness, *neuroses* and *psychoses*. A neurosis is an extreme fear or a violent desire that makes someone act in such a way that ordinary life becomes impossible. A housewife, for example, who develops a terror of leaving her home has a common neurosis called agoraphobia. This is a Greek word that means 'fear of the market place'. Obviously, if she is afraid to go out, she will become very unhappy and will find it more and more difficult to look after herself and her family. There are many other neuroses. They can be cured by specialists who help the sufferers understand how the fear began and how it can be overcome. Neuroses may have symptoms such as rapid heart beats, sweating or shakes, and special drugs called tranquilizers are sometimes used to control them.

Psychoses

Psychoses are serious mental illnesses. Psychotic persons cannot think or feel in an ordinary way. They may utterly believe some wild thing that is completely untrue, for example that invisible people are spying on them. Someone suffering

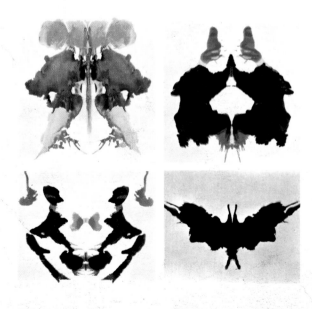

▶ A Swiss psychiatrist, Hermann Rorschach invented a test using ink blot patterns, some in black and white and some in colour. A person is shown each pattern and says what it brings to mind. The answers help the psychiatrist learn about emotions and fantasies a person might be too shy to talk about directly.

38

from this sort of illness can shift suddenly from being happy to being miserable enough to attempt suicide. Schizophrenia is the best known psychosis. People who suffer from it sometimes hear imaginary voices or see visions. They may become so ill they cannot move, speak or look after themselves in any way. For centuries, schizophrenia was the most dreaded mental illness. This was what most people meant when they said someone was insane. Now scientists believe that it may be caused by chemicals in the brain that have got out of balance. Drugs may restore the balance and the sufferers can be helped.

Helping the mentally ill

There are now many different sorts of specialist studying the human mind and caring for people with mental problems. Psychologists are those who concentrate on how the brain works and often work in laboratories. Some, called clinical psychologists, do their work with patients. Psychiatrists are medical doctors who have taken additional training in the field of mental illness. Psychotherapists, analysts and counsellors are all specialists with different training. They often work not just with those who are ill but with those who are in danger of becoming ill. They help people to come to a healthier and happier way of life.

Today, specialists who treat the mentally ill and those who look after the physically ill are working more closely together. Many diseases have psychosomatic elements. That means that the mind (*psyche*) and the body (*soma*) are acting on each other. If someone has a psychosomatic disease this does not mean that it is imaginary. It means that something in the person's mind is causing a very real problem in their body.

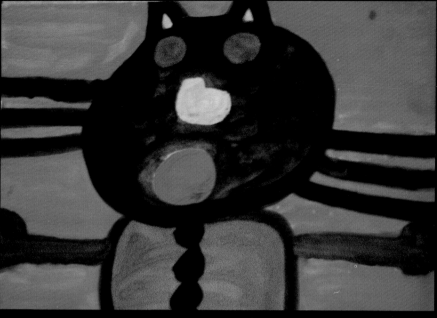

▲ Painting has become a very important part of the treatment, or therapy, given to people with mental illnesses. Often painting is the only way in which they can express themselves freely and so relieve the tensions of their illness.

▶ Vincent van Gogh, one of the most important painters at the end of the 19th century, suffered from periods of mental illness which were often reflected in the violent colours and brush-strokes of his paintings. In this self-portrait he has a bandage over his right ear because in one fit of madness he cut off his ear.

TOO MUCH OR TOO LITTLE

Sometimes our bodies give us trouble by making too much or too little of some important substance. Our skin has many tiny little holes called pores and through them we give off moisture to cool us when we are hot and tiny quantities of oil to keep the skin smooth. As our bodies slowly change from child to adult, our *hormones* sometimes cause too much oil to be made. This can block the pores and make us have spots. Occasionally, if the blockages are bad they cause a skin disease, acne. Sometimes the pancreas, an organ just in front of our kidneys, does not produce or use the right amount of the hormone insulin. When this happens, a person will suffer a disease called diabetes. There are many illnesses like this. Any disease that is caused by too little of something is called a deficiency disease. We can also get deficiency diseases through eating too little of the food our bodies need.

What sort of food we eat has a very great deal to do with how healthy we are. Babies and children need good food to grow and develop. Adults need it to stay healthy. Every day many parts of our

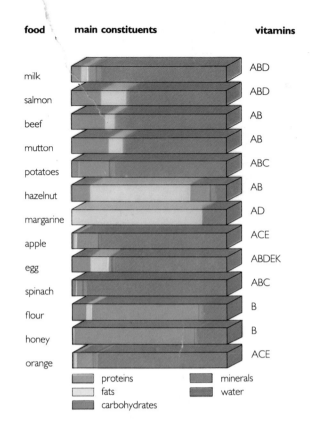

▲ A chart like this shows clearly which nutrients are present in several familiar foods. Notice how much of these foods is just water.

▶ A young girl who has diabetes is injecting herself with extra insulin so that the sugar she eats can be turned into useful energy instead of harming her. She injects the insulin rather than swallows it because powerful digestive juices would destroy the insulin before it entered her blood.

body are being repaired or replaced. The tiny white cells in our blood that are so important in protecting us from disease live for for only 13 days. New ones must be made constantly. All the special juices (enzymes) needed to digest what we eat must be made at each meal. Our skin is always rebuilding itself as the top layers flake away. But too much of the wrong food, or too little of the right food, will affect our health. But what is the 'right' food? Why can't we live on just chocolate and baked beans if we like them?

Different foods, different nutrients
A nutrient is something the body can absorb and use and all food contains one or more of the five basic nutrients. These nutrients are proteins, carbohydrates, fats, vitamins and minerals. Each is used by the body in a different way. Proteins are the building blocks. Every cell, no matter what sort it is, is made of protein. Important chemicals in the body such as

▲ Iodine is a mineral that is needed by the thyroid gland in our neck. If we do not get enough in our diet the gland becomes big and painful as it has for this man.

▶ This African child is suffering from near starvation. The stomach is bloated with gas, not food, and the hair is thin through lack of protein. Anyone who has been as short of a proper diet for as long as this child has little resistance to disease.

hormones and enzymes are made of protein. So are the antibodies that fight infection. Carbohydates are our chief energy supply. They provide fuel for the cells' work and all our actions. Fats give us more energy, some cell-building material and also act as the carriers for vitamins and minerals. Vitamins and minerals are special nutrients. We need very small amounts of many different sorts. Without each one, some important bodily process would go wrong.

Vitamins were given alphabetical names because when they were first discovered no one knew what they were. Vitamin A is needed for sight. The vitamin B group keeps the nerves and blood healthy. Vitamin C is used by the liver. There are many different vitamins and each has a special task. Minerals are very similar. Calcium, for example, is used in our bones and makes them strong.

Every food we eat has a different amount of nutrients. Some have traces of all five, but usually each food is mostly one type. Cream is mostly fat. Meat, fish and beans are largely protein. Vegetables are rich in vitamins and minerals. Bread and potatoes are full of carbohydrates. If we eat too much of one nutrient, we miss out on others. Sugar is pure carbohydrate. Although eating sweet things gives us energy, too many of them ruins our appetite for other nutrients.

▲ It may be healthy to be slim, but being too thin is just as unhealthy and bad for your body as being too fat. This woman has a condition called anorexia. People suffering from it are convinced they are fat, even though they are usually quite slim to start with. They eat less and less and may eventually starve themselves to death. Anorexia and severe overweight can both be signs that a person is unhappy, worried or anxious.

◄ This is the other extreme to the top picture and it is just as unhealthy. There are a few conditions that cause people to be as fat as this naturally, but they are very rare and most people are fat because they eat more than their body needs for the life they lead. A coal-miner, for example, doing hard physical work needs far more food than someone working at an office desk.

THE MOST IMPORTANT MUSCLE

If you run fast and stop suddenly you will feel a steady fast thumping in your chest. That is your heart, hard at work, pushing blood in and out of your lungs and round your body. Even when you are asleep, your heart keeps up its steady beating. Normally we never think about the way our heart works although it is the most important *muscle* in our body. If it stops, even for a short time, we die.

Basically, the heart is a tough muscle that surrounds four open spaces called chambers. Between the chambers and the tubes that let the blood in and out (*arteries* and *veins*) are what look like one-way swinging doors. These are the valves. As the heart muscle moves in and out, in a rippling effect, the chambers get larger and smaller, and the valves open and close. All that action pushes the blood along. It is pushed into the lungs where it deposits some waste material it has collected in the cells and picks up fresh oxygen which the cells need for life.

Many things can go wrong with this pumping system. We often hear people talking about 'heart trouble' and heart disease. Everyone is afraid of a 'heart attack'. What does it all mean?

Heart disease

There are two main sorts of heart disease: congenital – the kind people have from birth – and acquired. One baby out of every hundred is born with some sort of heart problem. Fortunately most of these are very slight. The heart muscle is formed during the first eight weeks of a baby's life inside its mother's body. Anything that affects the mother's health during that time, such as a poor diet, too much alcohol or smoking, can affect the way that muscle grows. Also sometimes the parents' genes, either the mother's or father's, may carry some information that makes the baby's cells develop in the wrong way. Modern medicine can help those babies a great deal. In some cases, the defect is small, just a tiny hole between two of the chambers perhaps. All the baby will need is careful examination to ensure that the hole will close

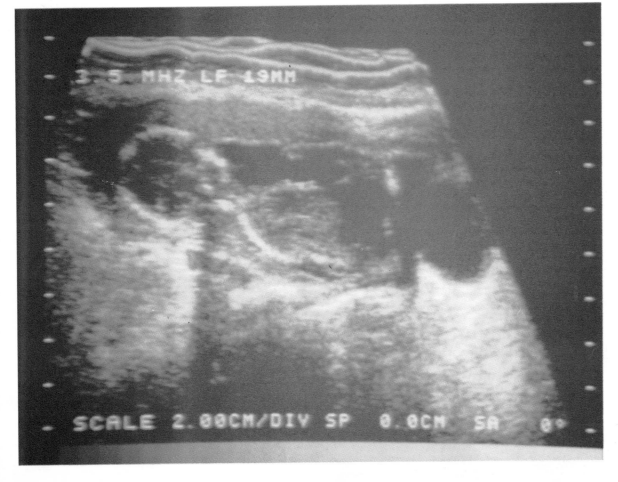

◄ Ultrasound is a modern method of detecting if there are medical problems inside a patient's body. Ultrasound scanning machines take 'pictures' of the inside of the body with sound waves. The 'pictures' the sound waves send back are shown on a television monitor screen. This ultrasound scan shows a baby inside its mother's womb – you can see the baby's head on the left of the scan. Although ultrasound equipment is expensive and complicated, the procedure for patients is very simple – if the scan is part of a routine check they do not have to stay in hospital and there is no anesthetic or surgery.

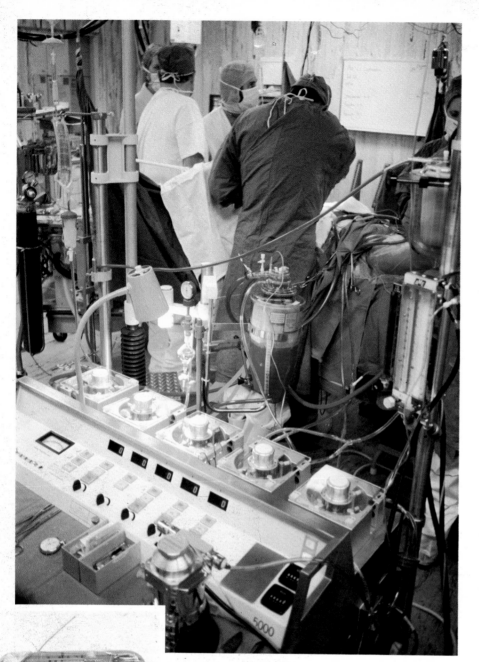

▲ Many operations were impossible until the invention of the heart-lung machine. The patient's blood supply is made to go through the machine not the heart. The machine (in the foreground of the picture) acts just like a heart: it keeps the patient's blood flowing, gives it essential oxygen and removes harmful carbon dioxide.

▲ This is a heart pacemaker fitted to patients whose hearts do not work properly. The four batteries provide the energy for the electric pulse that keeps the heart going. Some pacemakers work all the time, others at intervals. It depends on what is wrong with the heart.

damaged heart valves. They can even be replaced either with valves made from tissue or special plastic.

The arteries, the large tubes that carry oxygen-rich blood away from the heart, can become diseased as a person grows older. Gradually they become blocked by a kind of fatty material, much of which is a substance called cholesterol. The body needs cholesterol to build cells, but if too much is present in the blood it can damage the arteries. Sometimes bits of the blocking material break away and jam a tiny blood vessel. Sometimes the material irritates the wall of a blood vessel so much that it grows thin and eventually bursts like a balloon. If any part of the heart itself does not receive the blood it needs to carry on its work, it dies, just as other tissues in the body die. This is a myocardial infarction, the proper medical name for a common kind of heart attack. When two of the pumping chambers, the ventricles, cannot push through enough blood to keep the body going, a person has heart failure. Unless emergency help is on hand to keep circulation going until the heart takes up its regular beat again, the patient will die.

The heart muscle usually keeps going at a steady beat suitable for what the body is doing, slow when at rest, fast during work or exercise. Tiny electric pulses keep the muscles beating to time. Arrhythmia is a heart disease in which this beat becomes irregular. It can be corrected by drugs or, if serious, by a pacemaker. A pacemaker is a tiny instrument that checks the heart beat and when it goes wrong, supplies a tiny electric jolt to bring it back to its correct timing.

naturally as the heart grows. In other cases, the doctors can operate and correct the defect so the child grows up to have a normal, healthy life.

There are many forms of acquired heart disease. If a child or adult suffers an attack of rheumatic fever, their heart valves may be scarred and not work properly. Sometimes people have very mild rheumatic fever when they are young and the damage it has done to their hearts shows up only in middle age. However, operations can now repair

Preventing heart disease

A great deal of research is carried out in many countries to find out about heart disease, what causes it and how it can be prevented. Doctors now know that smoking, eating too much rich fatty food, heavy drinking and being overweight all make people more likely to suffer heart disease. Taking exercise and eating a good balanced diet are just two ways to help your heart stay healthy.

CANCER

Cancer is probably the most dreaded disease in the world tody. Doctors have known about it for centuries. Its name comes from an ancient Greek word meaning crab. Greek doctors noticed that cancer seemed to grab healthy tissue and hang on like a crab, eventually destroying it. More people are known to suffer cancer today than in the past but that is because other diseases, such as tuberculosis and pneumonia, have been conquered and people are now living longer. Cancer has taken their place as a major killer. In the past, doctors knew little about this mysterious disease that attacked many parts of the body in different ways. Powerful modern microscopes and other equipment have helped them understand their enemy.

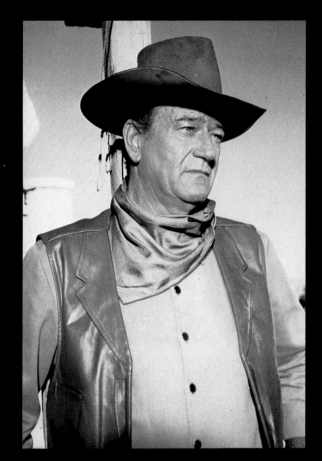

◀ Cancer can occur in anyone – young or old, male or female. Film star John Wayne died of cancer and in his last film played a character who knew that he, too, was dying of the disease.

◀ A photograph taken through an electron microscope shows what happens to a cancer cell when a patient is given a powerful anti-cancer chemical drug.

The cell wall is pitted and the cell is exploding and dying. Chemotherapy, as this treatment is called, is increasingly successful in treating the disease.

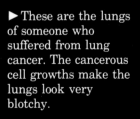

▶ These are the lungs of someone who suffered from lung cancer. The cancerous cell growths make the lungs look very blotchy.

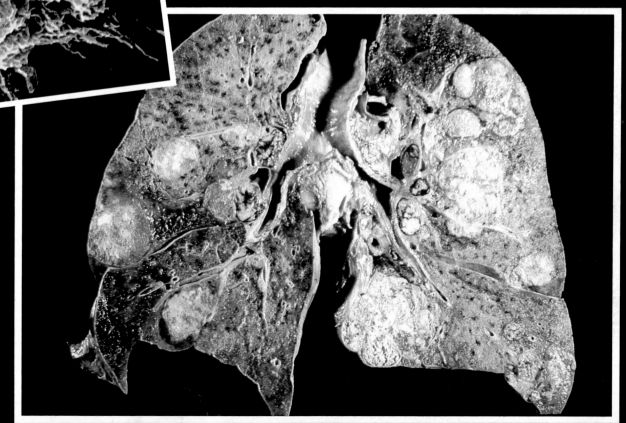

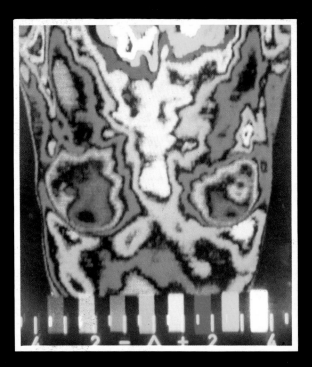

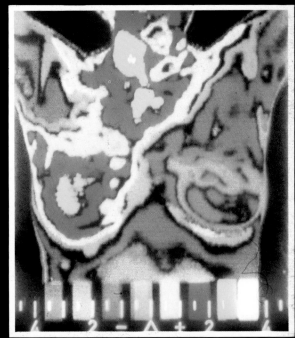

▶ Thermographs give 'pictures' of the body based on the temperature variations of the different parts. The colours indicate the temperature from white, the hottest, to dark blue, the coolest. On the **right** is a thermograph of a normal breast. The differences between it and the thermograph on the **far right** tells the doctor that the patient has breast cancer.

▶ **Right** These are healthy cells taken from the lining of the rectum, the very end of the large intestine, where waste is collected before leaving the body. You can see that the cells are in neat rows forming several little tubes. On the **far right** are the same types of cell from the same part of the body after they have been attacked by cancer. Only one or two little tubes remain. The cells are now jumbled and irregular. Obviously they cannot now perform their tasks correctly.

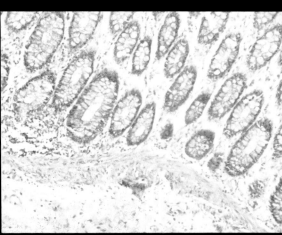
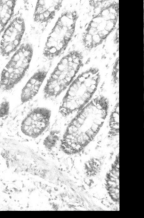

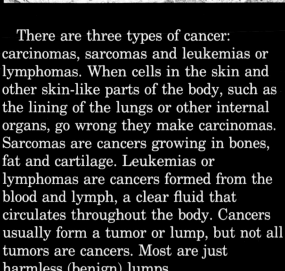

Danger – cells on the rampage

As we know, all the smallest parts of our body, our cells, are constantly growing, reproducing themselves, working, then dying and being replaced by new cells. This happens in an orderly way. Bone cells make bone cells. Red blood cells make red blood cells. Liver cells make liver cells and so on. When all parts of the body are working normally they make neither too many nor too few. Sometimes, however, something strange happens within a single cell. It starts to divide and makes more cells in a wild, haphazard way. The new cells are not like the other healthy ones. They do not do any work. They only make more and more of themselves, and they do it very much more quickly than other healthy cells. This is the beginning of a cancer.

There are three types of cancer: carcinomas, sarcomas and leukemias or lymphomas. When cells in the skin and other skin-like parts of the body, such as the lining of the lungs or other internal organs, go wrong they make carcinomas. Sarcomas are cancers growing in bones, fat and cartilage. Leukemias or lymphomas are cancers formed from the blood and lymph, a clear fluid that circulates throughout the body. Cancers usually form a tumor or lump, but not all tumors are cancers. Most are just harmless (benign) lumps.

Only a careful medical check can make sure which is which. In very dangerous cancers, harmful (malignant) cells flake off from the first tumor. They float through the body in the blood and then start their destructive work elsewhere. If cancer is not detected and treated quickly,

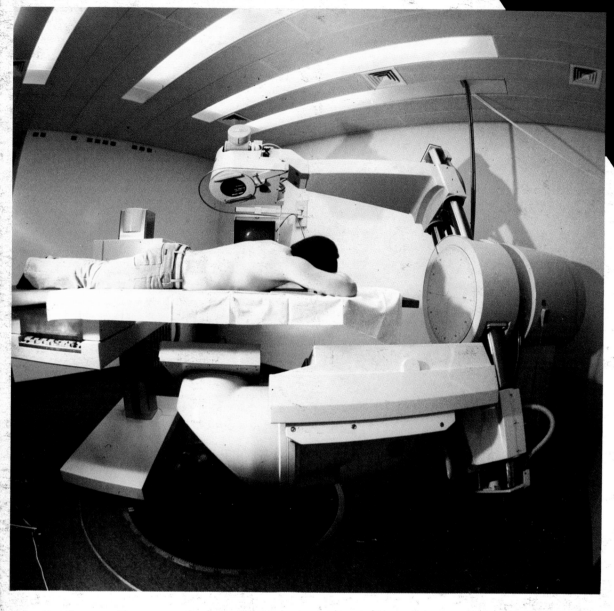

◄Cancer has not yet been conquered, but treatment for the disease is becoming more and more effective This patient is receiving radiation over the exact part of the body where the cancer is, to kill the cancer cells.

it will spread. Gradually it cuts off the work of healthy cells and the organs of the body fail.

Searching for a cure

Fortunately, the wonderful microscopes, radioactive material and other equipment that make it possible for doctors to study the disease also help them cure it. By examining small samples from within the body under powerful microscopes doctors can quickly tell if even the smallest quantity of cancer cells are at work. They can operate quickly to cut out malignant tumors and make certain they do not grow again. Powerful chemical drugs can kill some cancer cells without damaging healthy cells. Radiation is also used to kill diseased cells.

Doctors are hard at work trying to answer the question: what causes cancer?

They want to prevent it as well as cure it. They now know there are several causes, not just one. Cancer of the lungs, for example, is a type of cancer usually caused by a carcinogen. A carcinogen is a powerful chemical irritant. Carcinogens are present in cigarette smoke. Heavy smokers are often victims of lung cancer. Since the 1930s doctors have discovered hundreds of carcinogens. There are now laws to prevent such chemicals being used in dangerous quantities in food or agricultural products.

Some cancers seem to be caused by viruses so doctors are trying to discover which, as well as to find substances that will encourage the body to fight against them. Although controlled radiation cures cancer, uncontrolled radiation can cause it, especially leukemia, cancer of the blood.

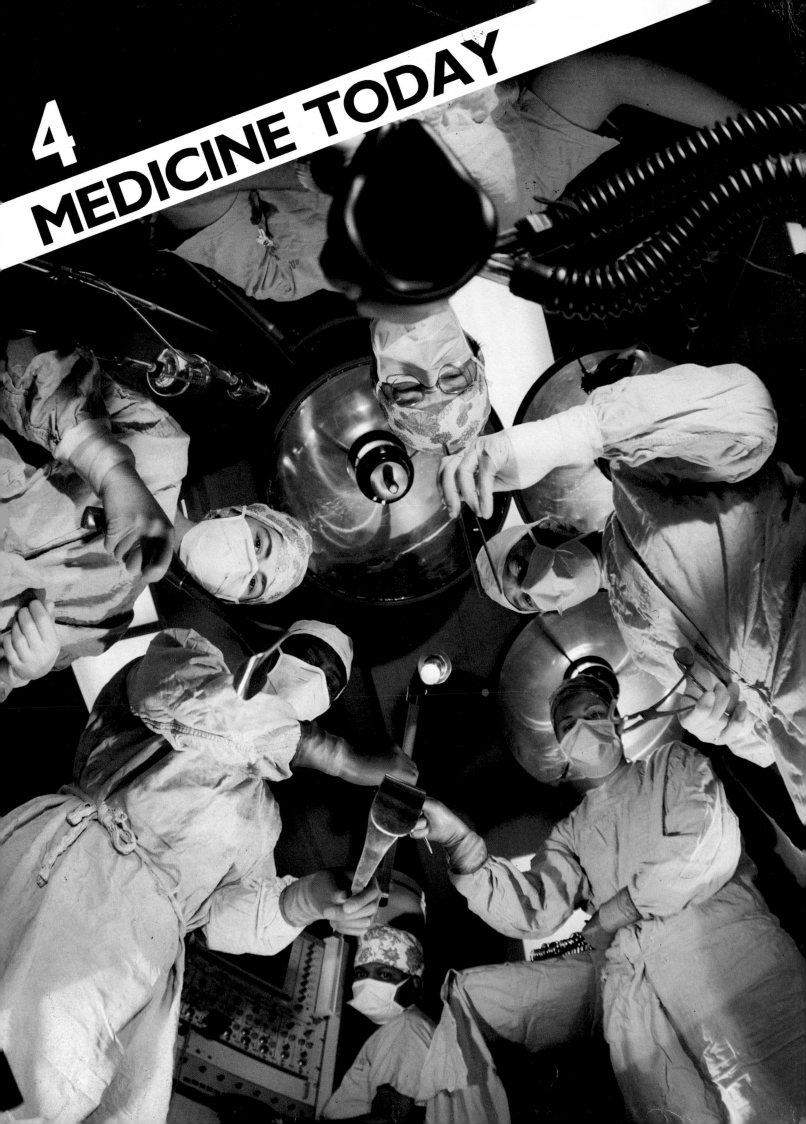

DOCTORS, THEIR TRAINING AND WORK

If by magic you found yourself at some great international meeting of doctors, you would learn a great deal about medicine just by looking around. Two or three thousand men and women from almost every nation on earth would be sitting in a hall listening to someone speak. Although they are all fully trained, very senior doctors, they come together to learn still more about some disease or health problem. A conference is a meeting that gives specialists a chance to catch up on the latest developments in their field. Even though they read about these things in their own magazines, called journals, they find it helpful to exchange ideas face to face. They know that no nation has all the good ideas. Large rich countries may have more money to spend on medical research than small, poorer countries, but that is no guarantee of good results.

At a big conference it is interesting to see how much doctors have in common, whatever differences there are in the politics of the countries they come from. Everywhere the training of new doctors is organized by experienced older doctors and is very similar. At school, students wanting to be doctors study as many science subjects as possible, especially chemistry, physics and biology. Then they go to study medicine either at a university or a medical school attached to a great hospital. As well as passing many difficult examinations, medical students must show the senior doctors that they have the right character to do the hard work and solve the difficult problems that make up a doctor's everyday work, because doctors really do make decisions that can mean life or death.

At a later stage in their training medical students watch and ask questions as patients are being treated by very experienced doctors. Students learn about diseases not just from books or from work in laboratories, but from watching doctors actually care for the sick. Even when students pass their final examinations, their training is not finished. They must spend some time working in a hospital under constant supervision by doctors with long experience. Only when this period is successfully over are they allowed to look after sick people on their own. Then, they can choose what kind of a doctor to be.

Different types of doctor

General *practitioners* are doctors who live in the community and see patients there. They form the basis of medical care for everyone. A general practitioner is the doctor who first sees you when you are ill. Some doctors decide they want to be surgeons. Surgeons perform operations. They cut into the body either to remove parts that are diseased or to repair injuries or other damage. A doctor who wants to be a surgeon must do more training to learn special skills. Some doctors decide that they want to concentrate on diseases that attack one part of the body, like the heart, eyes or brain. They too will do more studying and training to become specialists. Doctors who become interested in studying a

◄ A patient's-eye view of an operation, although few patients will actually see it like this because they will have had an anesthetic. Only one of these doctors will be the surgeon who is going to do the work. The others will have special jobs like checking that the anesthetic is not causing any side-effects. Others may be medical students who watch the operation to learn.

▼ Doctors learn basic scientific skills because sometimes they must be able to do tests on a patient's blood or other substances from the body if there are no laboratories nearby. Some doctors specialize in this sort of work. This one is examining some specimens through a microscope.

particular disease or trying to find some new treatment may go on to work in a laboratory and never see another patient after their first training is finished. Some doctors work in government offices, helping to plan projects to improve the country's general health. Doctors may work advising how to prevent disease, promote good nutrition or build hospitals. And other doctors, after their own long training is finished, may spend their time not only caring for the sick but also training others to become doctors and nurses.

NURSES

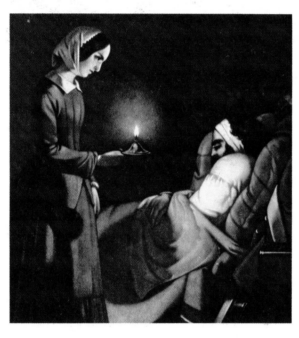

Today in medical schools around the world, men and women study together. In the past this was not so. Men alone were allowed to go to university or enter medical school. The only way a woman could help the sick was to become a nurse. Today's nurse, however, may even be a man. At first, men were not allowed to study nursing, just as women were not allowed to be doctors. Now both professions are open to men and women, so people can choose whichever suits their talents best.

Nurses look after the sick when they cannot care for themselves. They make sure the patients take the right amount of the correct drugs at the right time. They give them the sort of food that will help them get better. They watch and report changes in the patients' condition to the doctor. They help doctors give patients whatever special treatment they need. At all times nurses do their best to make sure patients are clean and comfortable.

In ancient times, these services to the sick were performed in the home, by the relatives of the sick person. In the early hospitals, these tasks were carried out by nuns, women who believed that by helping the sick they were serving God. Some nuns today still carry on that great tradition and dedicate their lives to caring for the sick, often in very remote and poor parts of the world.

Wars and revolutions that swept through Europe in the seventeenth and eighteenth centuries destroyed most of the old religious traditions of caring for the sick. Although doctors' training and skills continued to improve, that of nurses became worse and worse. By the 1860s nursing everywhere, except for a few groups of nuns, was a poor and terrible job that no-one wanted to do. Only those who were too ignorant or rough for anything better became nurses. Three inspiring people changed the picture in a very short time.

The beginnings of modern nursing
In Germany, in the early nineteenth century, Theodor Fliedner and his wife started a hospital and a small training centre called Kaiserwerth. They selected good and intelligent young women and taught them how to care for the very ill. When these women went to other hospitals the doctors appreciated that well-trained nurses really helped the sick to recover more quickly. In England, the woman who was to become the most famous nurse in the world, Florence Nightingale, heard about the work at Kaiserwerth. She had been interested in trying to help the sick for some time. She went to study with the Fliedners and also visited the Sisters of Charity in Paris, nuns who still practised good nursing skills. When England fought Russia in the Crimea, a part of southern Russia, Florence Nightingale was asked to go there to do something about the terrible army hospital at Scutari. More soldiers

▶ Florence Nightingale suggested that the sick be put in rows so that a nurse could easily check on many patients, especially during the night. The soldiers, grateful for her kind care, called her the 'Lady with the Lamp'.

◄Tribes that live in once isolated parts of the world often have little resistance to such illnesses as measles or even the common cold. As they come into increasing contact with people from more developed societies they are at great risk from such diseases. This nurse is a member of a health team that regularly visits remote villages in Papua New Guinea to monitor the health of the inhabitants.

were dying from disease and lack of care than from war wounds. In that hospital she began the work that forms the basis for modern nursing and the professional position nurses enjoy today. Women in many countries were inspired by her story. They copied her methods and founded professional nursing schools.

A modern nurse has an even more important role in the care of the sick than in the past. Modern medical treatment can use all sorts of machinery and very powerful drugs. A nurse must understand all this and be ready to carry out the doctor's instructions carefully and precisely. If a hospital has an 'intensive care unit' nurses will provide watchful supervision at every moment of the day and night. Nurses today will often work outside a hospital, too. They may work in community health care, visiting the sick in their homes. In some countries nurses will travel from village to village teaching people basic facts about health care.

▼In an intensive care unit, a very sick person will be attached to all sorts of electronic machines to tell the doctors what is happening deep inside his body. The nurse will be in charge of these machines and will have to intepret their information so that she can report to the doctors.

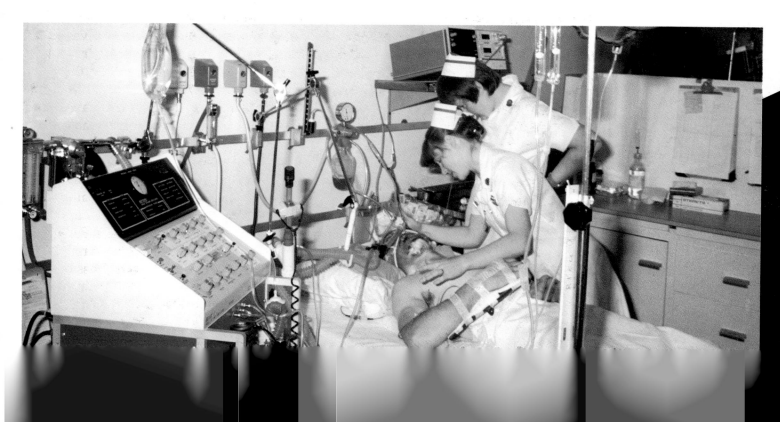

▲ A modern purpose-built hospital provides many different kinds of medical treatment and must also be flexible enough to cope with the victims of any sudden emergencies or disasters.

Hospitals are places where the sick go to receive special care and treatment that they cannot have in their own homes. Hospitals today come in all sizes. Big hospitals may look like a miniature town, with tower blocks for special departments. Hospitals often have lovely gardens where the sick can have peace, comfort and quiet, just as the ancient Greeks advised. But hospitals can also be ugly old buildings, uncomfortable to work in, set in the middle of noisy, dirty cities. In some parts of the world, a hospital is just a hut. Sometimes a hospital is a huge Red Cross truck full of medical equipment, providing emergency care somewhere where disaster has struck. Even airplanes and ships can be hospitals for wounded soldiers in war.

Different parts of a hospital
In a big hospital there are many different parts working together to help the many people who need all sorts of different medical care. Usually we think of a hospital as a place where people go for operations and everything to do with surgery certainly takes up a great deal of space in a hospital. Near the main entrance of a large hospital there is often a special emergency entrance, where *ambulances* take people who have

suddenly become very ill, perhaps with a heart attack or injuries from a car accident. Close to an emergency department there may be a special room for operations, ready day and night for the unexpected, unplanned operation.

Other operating rooms in a hospital will be used according to a well-planned schedule. Patients will come on a special day, be prepared and know what is to be done. These operating rooms may have television equipment as well as all the medical equipment the doctors need. Television is used so that students who are training to be surgeons can watch operations without having to go through the long preparation of dressing themselves in sterile clothing so they can watch the operation as the surgeon does it.

Patients will be either in rooms on their own or sharing with two or three others. In some of the older hospitals they may be in very large rooms with many other patients. These rooms are called wards. Usually hospitals group together patients who are having the same sort of treatment. There will also be a special section for new mothers and babies – the maternity department. Patients with dangerous or infectious disease will be kept in a separate section or in 'isolation', well away from other people.

During the day, some people come to the hospital just for a short visit to see one of the senior specialists or to receive some special treatment or test. Doctors

▶ The heart of a modern hospital is its operating rooms (**top**). These are carefully planned so that the surgeon will find everything helpful for his work. Even the air is specially filtered so it will be sterile – germ free. Everything around the operating room (**below**) will also be planned so that the area can be kept as clean and germ free as possible.

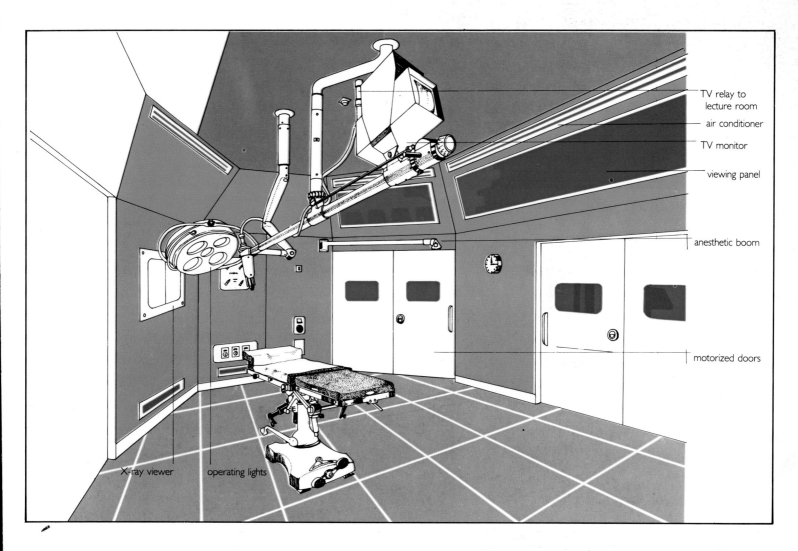

TV relay to
lecture room
air conditioner
TV monitor
viewing panel
anesthetic boom
motorized doors

X-ray viewer   operating lights

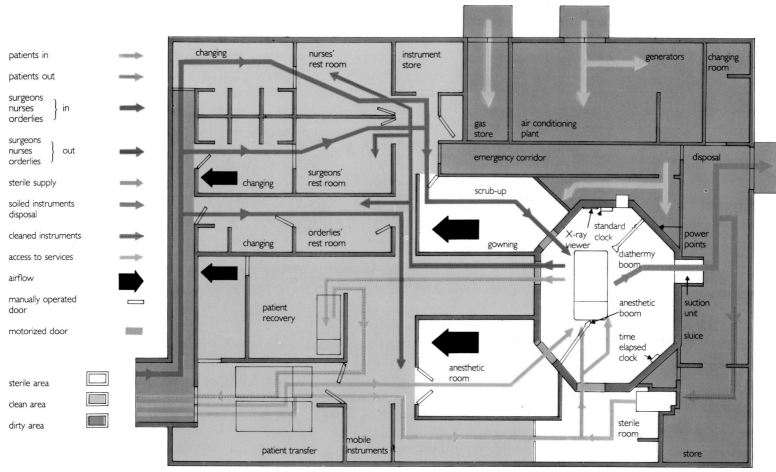

patients in
patients out
surgeons
nurses } in
orderlies
surgeons
nurses } out
orderlies
sterile supply
soiled instruments
disposal
cleaned instruments
access to services
airflow
manually operated
door
motorized door

sterile area
clean area
dirty area

changing   nurses'   instrument   generators   changing
                  rest room   store   room

                                                           gas   air conditioning
                                                           store   plant

                                       emergency corridor   disposal

            changing   surgeons'   scrub-up
                        rest room
                                                                                  standard
                                                                      X-ray   clock   power
            changing   orderlies'   gowning   viewer   points
                        rest room   diathermy
                                                                              boom
                                                                                                  suction
                                                                              anesthetic   unit
                        patient   boom
                        recovery   time
                                                                              elapsed   sluice
                                                                              clock
                                          anesthetic
                                          room
                                                                                                  sterile
                                                                                                  room

              patient transfer   mobile   store
                                 instruments

53

▶ These pictures give you an idea of the different sorts of medical care that can be happening in a hospital at any time.
1 A pregnant mother is having a scan to make sure that her baby is healthy – you can see the baby clearly on the right-hand screen.
2 A doctor checks the progress of a new-born baby in the intensive care unit. **3** A doctor examines a child in the out-patients department.

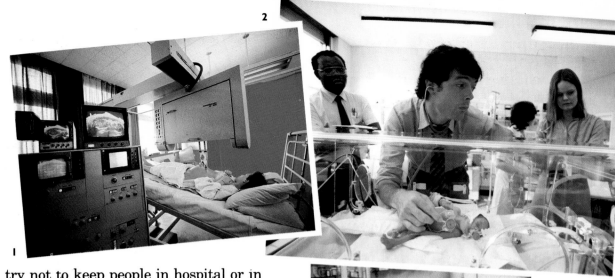

try not to keep people in hospital or in bed for more than a short time. They know a person gets well more quickly at home, surrounded by familiar faces and things.

Doctors and nurses are not the only people working in the hospital day and night. Cooking, cleaning, repair to vital electrical equipment, telephones, communication systems – everything has to be perfect all the time. Lives depend on all the parts working together smoothly.

RESEARCH AND THERAPY

Doctors and nurses are not the only highly-trained people who work in hospitals and medical centres to help the sick. Chemists, physicists and biologists often work in research laboratories there trying to discover and test new drugs. Any substance that may be helpful is investigated. Because some animals like pigs and monkeys have body systems similar to our own, scientists know that if a drug is safe when given to them, it probably will be safe for us too. Computers and other electronic equipment help speed up research work and make checks and tests more precise.

Hospitals have laboratories because they need them for their regular work as well as for research. Because the early stages of many illnesses can seem very similar, a doctor will ask for a check, or analysis, of a patient's blood, some other body fluid or even perhaps a small piece of tissue in order to be sure what disease is at work. Other analyses will be made to check on how treatment is progressing.

Sometimes tests must be done very quickly if emergency treatment is needed.

Therapists at work
Other specialists working in a hospital or health centre often have 'therapist' as part of their title. Therapy means healing treatment and a therapist is someone who gives it. Speech therapists work patiently with those who cannot speak or have serious problems with speaking. A child may be born with a speech defect. An adult may loose the ability to speak either because of an illness, such as a stroke, or because of an accident.

Physiotherapists are very busy people in modern hospitals. They give a wide variety of treatments to patients of all ages to help them use their bodies normally. If someone has an illness that causes paralysis, so that part of the body cannot be moved, the physiotherapist may have to massage it so that the muscles do not become weak and useless. If someone has an amputation, that is an operation

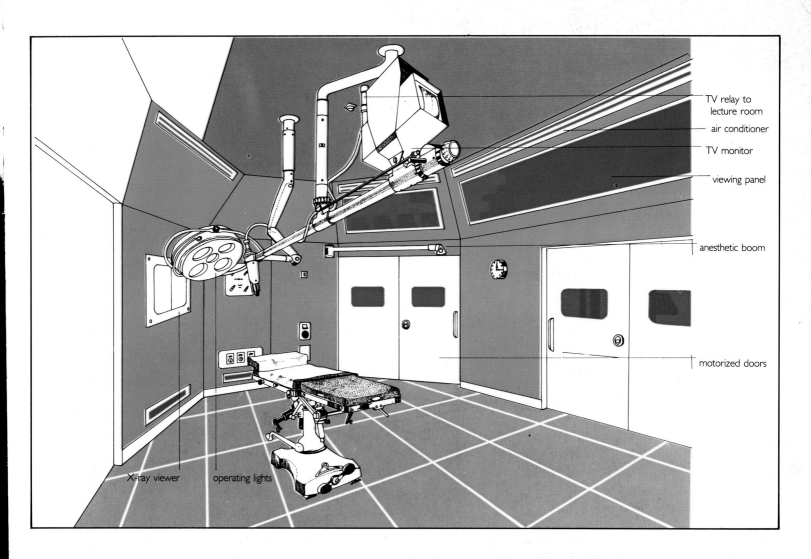

TV relay to lecture room

air conditioner

TV monitor

viewing panel

anesthetic boom

motorized doors

X-ray viewer   operating lights

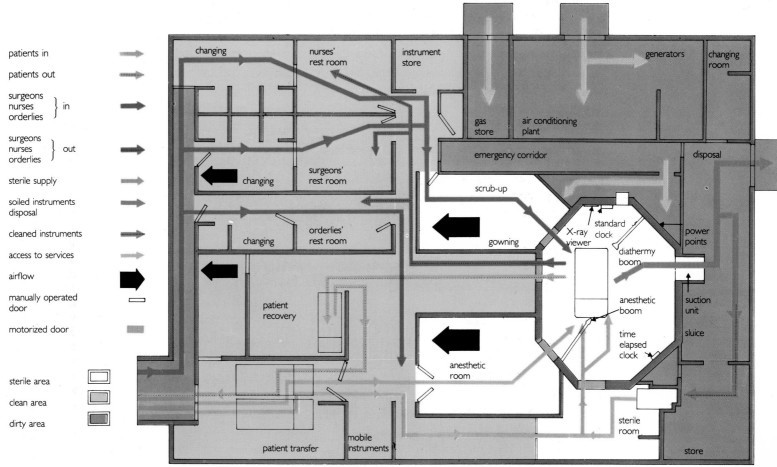

patients in

patients out

surgeons
nurses } in
orderlies

surgeons
nurses } out
orderlies

sterile supply

soiled instruments
disposal

cleaned instruments

access to services

airflow

manually operated
door

motorized door

sterile area

clean area

dirty area

changing   nurses'   instrument   generators   changing
                  rest room   store   room

                                                    gas   air conditioning
                                                    store   plant

                                                    emergency corridor   disposal

changing   surgeons'   scrub-up
                  rest room

                                                                          standard
                                                                          clock
changing   orderlies'   gowning   X-ray   power
                  rest room   viewer   diathermy   points
                                                                    boom

                                                                    anesthetic   suction
patient   boom   unit
recovery
                                                                                      sluice
                                                          time
                                                          elapsed
                                                          clock
                                   anesthetic
                                   room
                                                                                      sterile
                                                                                      room

patient transfer   mobile   store
                   instruments

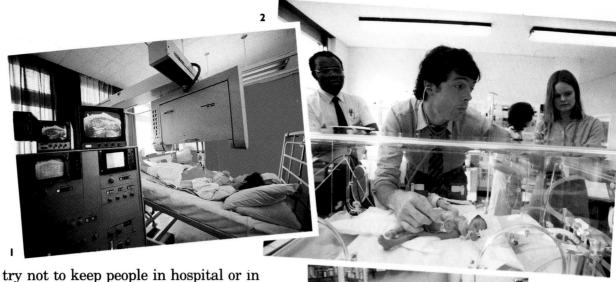

▶ These pictures give you an idea of the different sorts of medical care that can be happening in a hospital at any time.
1 A pregnant mother is having a scan to make sure that her baby is healthy – you can see the baby clearly on the right-hand screen.
2 A doctor checks the progress of a new-born baby in the intensive care unit. 3 A doctor examines a child in the out-patients department.

try not to keep people in hospital or in bed for more than a short time. They know a person gets well more quickly at home, surrounded by familiar faces and things.

Doctors and nurses are not the only people working in the hospital day and night. Cooking, cleaning, repair to vital electrical equipment, telephones, communication systems – everything has to be perfect all the time. Lives depend on all the parts working together smoothly.

RESEARCH AND THERAPY

Doctors and nurses are not the only highly-trained people who work in hospitals and medical centres to help the sick. Chemists, physicists and biologists often work in research laboratories there trying to discover and test new drugs. Any substance that may be helpful is investigated. Because some animals like pigs and monkeys have body systems similar to our own, scientists know that if a drug is safe when given to them, it probably will be safe for us too. Computers and other electronic equipment help speed up research work and make checks and tests more precise.

Hospitals have laboratories because they need them for their regular work as well as for research. Because the early stages of many illnesses can seem very similar, a doctor will ask for a check, or analysis, of a patient's blood, some other body fluid or even perhaps a small piece of tissue in order to be sure what disease is at work. Other analyses will be made to check on how treatment is progressing.

Sometimes tests must be done very quickly if emergency treatment is needed.

Therapists at work

Other specialists working in a hospital or health centre often have 'therapist' as part of their title. Therapy means healing treatment and a therapist is someone who gives it. Speech therapists work patiently with those who cannot speak or have serious problems with speaking. A child may be born with a speech defect. An adult may loose the ability to speak either because of an illness, such as a stroke, or because of an accident.

Physiotherapists are very busy people in modern hospitals. They give a wide variety of treatments to patients of all ages to help them use their bodies normally. If someone has an illness that causes paralysis, so that part of the body cannot be moved, the physiotherapist may have to massage it so that the muscles do not become weak and useless. If someone has an amputation, that is an operation to remove part or all of an arm or leg, the physiotherapist will play an important part in teaching the person how to use a prosthesis, or artificial limb. Sometimes physiotherapy treatment is given in a special warm swimming pool where gently moving water helps patients to stand and move easily by themselves.

Psychotherapists help people recovering from mental illness. They may help patients perform some easy work or enjoyable game to give them new confidence in themselves. A psychotherapist may also organize a group activity for several patients. It takes a great deal of skill and understanding to get worried and frightened patients to relax and co-operate with each other, but this helps them get well.

Radiotherapy is another important type of modern medical treatment. We usually think of plutonium, cobalt and uranium as deadly substances used in bombs. However, they can also be used to heal the sick instead of kill. The radiotherapist aims the radiation on to a diseased part of the body and it kills the harmful cells. Cancer patients often go back to hospital after an operation to receive radiotherapy. This ensures that the cancer cells will not grow again.

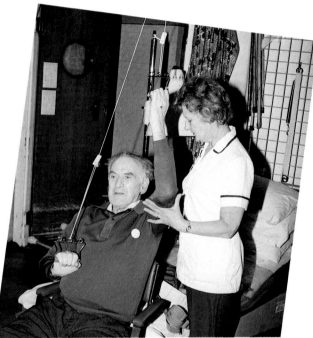

◀Physiotherapy after an operation (**left**) is very important. It helps to strengthen weak muscles. The patients (**below**) are not just enjoying themselves, they are having physiotherapy. The water helps support bodies weakened by illness.

SURGERY

▼ A tray of surgical instruments used during the 18th century.

Surgery is the branch of medicine that helps patients either by removing some diseased part of the body, or else by replacing or repairing it. This happens during an operation performed by a specially trained doctor who is a surgeon.

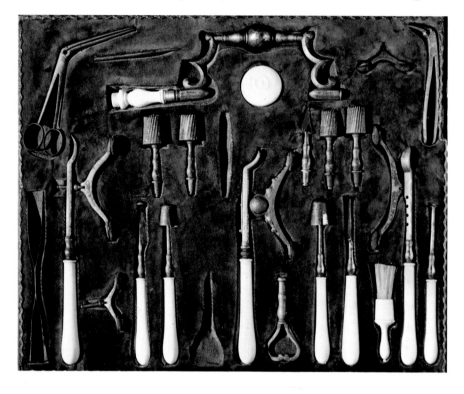

Nowadays, because operations are possible on all parts of the body, including the brain, surgeons usually specialize in only one area: the eye, the heart, the kidneys or the bones, for example. A general surgeon will perform the fairly straightforward and common operations such as appendectomy – a removal of the appendix, a small sac attached to the bowel which may become infected and even burst.

Until fairly recently, surgeons could safely remove only a few parts of the body, such as an injured arm or leg, the tonsils or the appendix. Now it is possible to control infections and even make replacement parts for the body out of plastic or metals that will not be affected by the body's own chemicals. This means that surgeons can do much more. In a team, working with other experts such as anesthetists, they can open up the chest of a newly-born baby and actually sew up a hole in its heart. When the child recovers the heart will grow and heal normally. Surgeons can operate on an old person who cannot walk because the big joint

▶ This diagram shows some of the instruments a modern surgeon would use in his work. Unlike the ones above, they are all made of steel and are easy to sterilize. Each type of instrument comes in a variety of shapes and sizes because of the different types of work the surgeons have to do in different parts of the body. The top two clamps, for example are non-crushing. They are used to lift soft tissues and intestines without damage. The lower two are designed to crush tissue to stop bleeding, say.

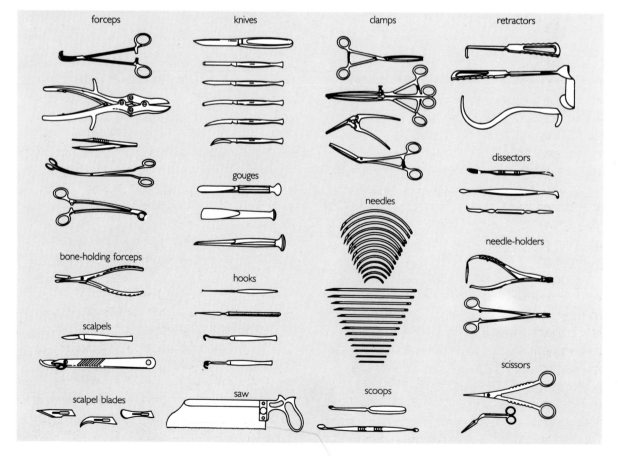

where the leg fits into the hip has become damaged by the disease, arthritis. The damaged joint is taken out of the body and replaced by a man-made one that will work smoothly. Eye surgeons can save the sight of people who have been injured by broken glass in an accident. They can also remove a cataract, a grey membrane that sometimes forms in the lens of the eye causing blindness. They can even restore sight to a blind person by giving him or her a part of the eye of someone who has died.

These operations are possible because of the new understanding about how important germ-free atmosphere is, how a patient must be kept free from pain but breathing steadily with a good supply of blood, how drugs can be used to make sure the body recovers quickly from the strain of the operation.

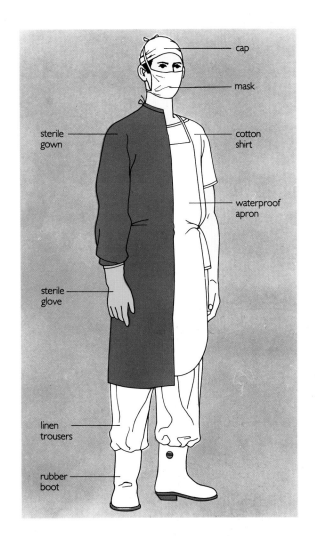

▶ A surgeon prepared for an operation wears special sterile clothes to be sure that he does not transfer any harmful germs to the patient. The garments are loose and comfortable because sometimes operations can take many hours.

TRANSPLANTS

The most spectacular recent victories in medicine's battle against disease have been in surgery. Everyone has heard about heart transplants. But people often do not know that some forms of transplant have been a part of medical treatment for a long time. Two hundred years ago, doctors learned how to make skin taken from one part of a patient's body grow to cover a wound or burn on another part. This was the first transplant.

Later, when doctors tried to take skin from one person, a donor, and give it to another, this did not work. They had to experiment for a long time before they understood why it did not work. First the problem of infection from germs had to be overcome. Then it was necessary to understand how the body's immune system worked. Surgeons now know that if a patient is not properly prepared by

drugs, the body will reject the transplant. That is, the cells in the body will automatically start producing antibodies to destroy the new tissue, just as if it were made of harmful germs. Now surgeons can perform a whole variety of transplants because new drugs suppress a patient's immune reaction and give the new tissue time to become accepted.

Transplanting kidneys
One of the most successful types of transplant operation is kidney replacement. The kidneys are the important organs that constantly filter the blood and remove waste from it. Although you can live quite normally if one kidney is removed or damaged by disease, you will die very quickly if the other fails. At first, surgeons replaced a diseased kidney only if they could take one from a healthy member of the

patient's own close family. They knew that the new kidney had to 'match' the old one very closely or, even with drugs, it would soon be rejected in its new body. Gradually a new system of matching body tissues called tissue-typing was developed. This made it possible for surgeons to use kidneys from other donors and even kidneys from people who had recently died. Today many people carry cards to say they are willing to have parts of their body used in this way when they die. This is a great help to medicine because often surgeons can use parts of the body of a person killed in an accident to help others, if permission is given quickly after death.

Other kinds of transplants

Bone can also be transplanted and so can parts of the eye. The cornea, the transparent window at the front of the eye, can be removed from a dead person and given to a patient who is blind. The new cornea will enable the person to see again.

Heart transplants are the most spectacular of all. They involve a large team of surgeons and other specialists. Special life-support machines actually do the work of the heart and lungs of the patient while the operation is going on. Very few of the thousands of people who suffer from serious heart disease are likely to have the chance of a transplant. It helps only some types of heart disease and the person to receive the new heart must be otherwise fit and healthy. It is also very difficult to obtain a donor heart in good condition at the right time.

DENTISTRY

Few of us will need the help of a heart surgeon in our life but all of us should see a dentist regularly. Dentists are an important part of the medical profession. They provide constant care for our teeth, a most important part of our body. The teeth begin preparing the food we eat for digesting. If they are sore and painful we may stop eating good, wholesome food and just eat soft, sweet things that are easy to swallow. Poor nutrition can harm us in

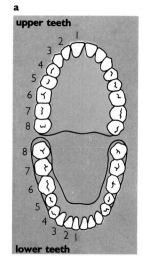

▼ These two charts show you how a healthy adult's teeth are arranged in the mouth. Thirty-two teeth make up two rows **a**, the top and bottom do not meet exactly because the sharp front teeth cut food like the blades of a scissors and the flatter back teeth grind the food. When you see a tooth out of the mouth, as in the chart **b** it is easy to tell what sort of job it does. The long finger-like parts are the roots that go down into the jaw. Incisors are used for cutting, canines for tearing, premolars and molars for grinding.

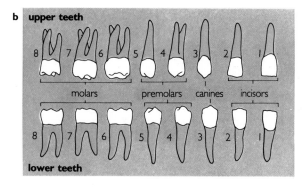

many ways. When teeth become diseased they can be very painful. Bad teeth can even cause the whole body to be infected by harmful bacteria that form in and around them in the mouth. Sometimes serious dental problems can only be cured by an operation. Many dentists, therefore, are also trained as surgeons.

Caries, tooth decay, is the main disease that attacks teeth. It is caused by bacteria that feed on the tiny bits of food trapped between or on the surface of the teeth after we eat. As they feed, these bacteria make an acid. The acid slowly dissolves the hard white enamel that covers the outer visible part of the tooth. If caries is not diagnosed and treated quickly the hole gets larger and larger. It also eats deeper into the tooth. When it reaches sensitive parts of the tooth, such as the dentine layer, the tooth begins to ache. Later caries may spread into the pulp of the tooth and down into the root. The infection can spread to other parts of the body and can be so serious it must be treated by antibiotics.

In the dentist's chair

When you make your regular visit to the dentist, your teeth will be checked for any early sign of caries. Holes will be cleaned and then filled with a substance that will not decay. The dentist also checks to make sure your gums, the pink tissue around the visible base of the teeth, are healthy. Gum diseases, which are often caused by poor hygiene or bad diet, can damage the teeth and may be symptoms of other health problems.

Modern dentists have many ways of repairing and replacing teeth. Cleaning out all the bits of a decayed tooth can be done very quickly with high speed drills

dental operations are usually carried out just like other operations. Then, the patient may be given a general anesthetic and be completely unconscious while the work is done.

X-ray photography is a great aid to the dentist. It is used to check that children's teeth are growing properly. Later it can reveal hidden problems in the roots of the teeth that go down into the jawbone. X-rays help a dental surgeon if he has to repair any damage to a person's teeth or jaws caused by an accident. Dentists, too, are experimenting with transplants, to replace teeth damaged by injury or disease. False teeth made of plastic or porcelain look so natural they are almost impossible to detect. But dentists would rather their patients cleaned their teeth regularly and avoided sugary foods.

▼ Our modern diet is so full of sugary foods and drinks that daily teeth-cleaning and regular visits to the dentist are extremely important if we are to keep our teeth healthy. This girl is having a routine check to ensure that her teeth are free from holes.

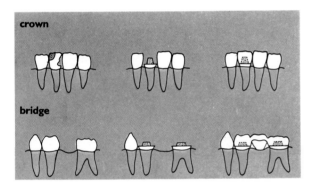

crown

bridge

▲ Sometimes a dentist must replace only part of a damaged tooth or fit just one false tooth in between other teeth so a person can chew food easily. Here are two common repairs. When a tooth is crowned, the diseased part is drilled away and a clean stump is left on top of the still healthy roots. The dentist then cements a porcelain crown to this and the tooth has the shape and colour of a normal tooth. With a bridge, the teeth on either side of a gap are crowned with gold or platinum and then the false tooth is anchored between them. Gold or platinum are used because they are strong and are not affected by the body's chemicals or food.

that make little noise and are cooled by water so they cause hardly any discomfort. The dentist can choose from many different types of drug to make sure the patient feels no pain. For simple procedures, perhaps only a mild tranquilizer is needed, or an anesthetic that takes the feeling away from a small portion of the mouth and jaw. Serious

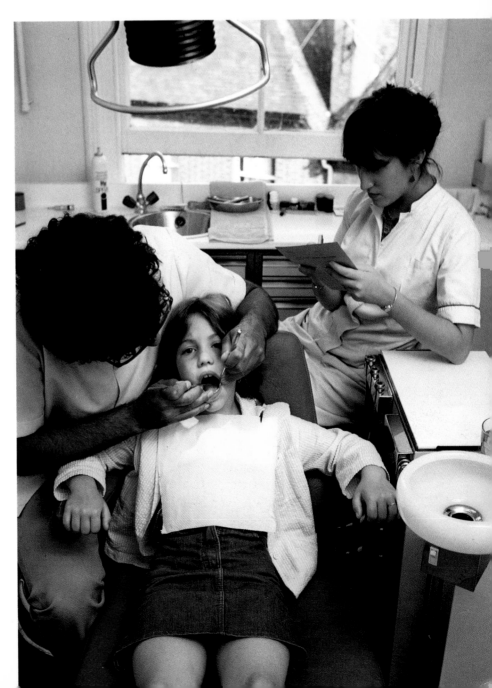

MEDICINE'S ENEMIES TODAY

The story of vaccinations, wonder drugs, transplant operations, X-rays, heart and lung machines, hospitals the size of small towns – all these amazing developments can mislead us into thinking that medicine is one great success story. But this is not true, as any doctor will quickly admit. Some of the problems are easy to see.

There are still many serious diseases like cancer or multiple sclerosis that are mysterious and difficult to cure. Curing diseases can sometimes create new medical problems. A health team can vaccinate everyone in a remote part of a poor country. The people will then not die of cholera or typhoid. They may die of malnutrition instead.

In rich Western countries, good medical treatment means that more and more people are living to seventy, eighty, or even ninety years or more. This means that doctors must spend more and more time dealing with the diseases that attack the body as it wears out from old age. Hospitals must try to care for an increasing number of elderly patients whose families cannot look after them. At the other end of life, new treatments and machines save the lives of tiny babies that, twenty or thirty years ago, would have died at birth or soon after. Now these children live, but some will have health problems throughout their lives. Their parents may be unable or unwilling to care for them.

A new kind of disease

Doctors today are particularly worried about what are called 'iatrogenic' diseases. These can be anything from rashes or stomach disorders to severe muscular pain or birth defects in a newborn child. These are illnesses that a patients gets as a result of being treated for something else. Many of the powerful life-saving drugs have serious side-effects. Although everything is done to find out about these while the drugs are still being tested and before they are used, sometimes the problems do not become obvious until the drug has been used for some time. Even some kinds of treatment, perhaps one which involves a person staying in hospital for a long time, can do damage because later the patient will find it hard to adjust to life outside hospital.

Problems of modern times

Modern life itself creates medical problems. People in crowded, noisy, dirty cities doing boring uninteresting jobs easily develop habits such as smoking, drinking or overeating that damage their health. Depression and drug abuse are difficult to help medically.

Doctors are concerned that even their successes and the treatments they have available may sometimes frighten sick people and make them reluctant to come forward when they need help. They know, too, that as their profession becomes more and more specialized, making a good diagnosis that considers the whole person becomes more difficult instead of easier.

The final enemy of medical progress today is the cost of good care and research. New drugs are expensive. New machines for diagnosis and treatment are constantly being developed, each more expensive than the last. In some countries, good medical care is expensive and not easily available. In others, it may be supplied free but is paid for by heavy taxes. Health care can become a political issue.

▲ Jacqueline du Pré, the world-famous cello player, developed multiple sclerosis. Unable to play any more, she has bravely turned to teaching.

▼ Heart transplant operations have brought new life to many people suffering from what, until very recently, were incurable heart diseases. Keith Castle had a successful transplant.

MEDICINE IN THE FUTURE

It is difficult to guess where medicine will have its next triumphs. Perhaps 'spare part' surgery really will become common if scientists can make safe and efficient minature machines to do the work of diseased hearts, livers or kidneys. Perhaps as more is learned about encouraging the body's immune response, vaccinations will be a thing of the past. A single injection might be all that is needed to encourage our own antibodies to fight off all invaders, even the common cold! As the causes of diseases are understood, the chances to develop cures increase.

Preventing illness is certain to become a key job in medicine. Some of this will happen through education. As children and adults learn more about how their bodies work and how to take good care of them, diseases that flourish because of ignorance and neglect will become less common.

Medicine is sure to be an important partner in space research. Astronauts have to be fit and healthy before they take off and they have to stay that way in space. Space stations will provide wonderful laboratories where scientists can carry out medical experiments that cannot be done on earth because of atmospheric pressure and gravity. Perhaps in time some diseases will be treated in space.

Computers and other forms of electronic technology certainly will play an important part in future medicine. In fifty years time, equipment in an operating room may be as different from today's as today's is from that used in the Middle Ages. The only thing we can be sure about is that in 2001, the men and women training for the medical profession will learn how to use the marvellous machines and the amazing drugs. They also will learn, like all doctors since the time of Hipppocrates, to look, listen, observe and diagnose. They are sure to be reminded of how human, ancient and honorable is their profession of caring for the sick.

▲ Some people, worried about the side-effects of some modern drugs, have turned to old herbal cures or other unorthodox systems of 'medicine'. Wise doctors keep open minds and explore all avenues, because anything that helps in the fight against disease is useful, wherever it comes from.

GLOSSARY

Acids Strong chemicals that can make other substances dissolve.

Allergen Substance that makes the body produce antibodies in the blood, just as if there were germs present, so causing an allergy.

Allergy Unpleasant and unusual reaction to something that is normally harmless.

Ambulance A special vehicle to take very sick people to hospital quickly.

Analgesic Drug that reduces pain without affecting a person in other ways.

Anatomy The science of how the human body is made.

Anesthetic Something that takes away the power of feeling. In large quantities it can cause unconsciousness.

Antibiotic Substance that can destroy organisms such as germs.

Antibody Protein made by the blood to destroy germs entering the body.

Antigen Another name for allergen.

Antiseptic Substance that will act against sepsis (infection).

Arteries Tubes in the body that carry oxygen-rich blood away from the heart.

Arthritis Inflammation of the joints.

Bacteriology The science of bacteria.

Bacterium (plural **bacteria**) Small organism(s) that often cause diseases.

Cells The basic unit of life. They feed, grow, reproduce themselves and die. Different types of cells in the body do different work.

Chemicals A basic substance out of which others can be made.

Childbirth Having a baby.

Colony A group of bacteria living together in one place.

Congenital Something that is with you from birth. A congenital illness is one you were born with.

Contagious Something, usually a disease, that is spread from one person to another by close physical contact.

Contaminate To infect with a disease.

Diagnosis When a doctor identifies a patient's illness from a study of the symptoms.

Dissection The careful cutting open of dead bodies to learn about the parts of the body beneath the skin.

Epidemic Disease common in a certain area at a certain time.

Examination Looking at something or someone in a planned, scientific way.

Gland Organ in the body that secretes (gives out) a special substance.

Hormones Chemical messengers in the blood.

Host Plant or animal that is lived on by a parasite.

Immune/immunity When an organism is safe from getting a disease.

Infect/infection Pass on a disease; a disease.

Inflamed Red, swollen and painful.

Muscle Tissue that is made up of fibres, strands like thread. It can grow long or short, expand or contract.

Neurosis (plural **neuroses**) Type of

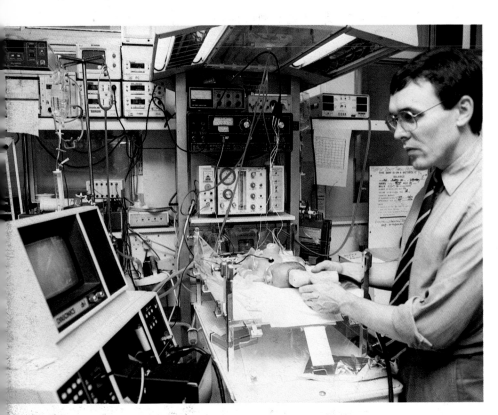

▼ A tiny baby in an intensive care unit is attached to a number of machines to check that his body is working properly.

◀All these pins and bolts can be put into the body to repair damaged bones or joints. A badly broken arm or leg will be pinned together by a surgeon and will then be able to heal.

mental illness in which the patient has such violent fears or wishes that normal life is impossible.

Oxygen An invisible gas that all living things need constantly in order to stay alive.

Parasite A living organism that lives on or in and feeds on another living organism. In humans parasites frequently cause diseases.

Physical Anything to do with things we can see, touch, taste, smell and feel; anything to do with our bodies.

Physiology The science of how the living body works.

Practitioner A doctor. Having a job as a doctor is called practising.

Psychosis (plural **psychoses**) Severe mental illness affecting the patient's whole character.

Quarantine Period of time when someone who may have been in contact with a serious disease is kept away from other people to try to stop the disease spreading.

Rash A rough painful redness of the skin.

Research Working on a problem in a systematic scientific way.

Sewers Underground pipes that carry dirty water away from the baths, sinks and toilets of houses and other buildings.

Skeleton The bones which act as support for the rest of the body.

Specialist A person with a great deal of detailed knowledge of one subject.

Symptoms Outward signs or feelings that show the body is not working properly.

Tissue A group of cells from one part of the body.

Treatment What is done to help a sick person get better.

Unconscious Not being able to see or move and totally unaware of what is happening to you.

Vaccination Giving a living organism immunity from a serious disease by deliberately giving a mild form of the disease.

Veins Tubes in the body that carry blood back to the heart.

Virus Minute organism that can cause disease.

▼ Children need to play whether they are in hospital or not. Play is now recognized as being important to a child's recovery from illness or an operation. Children's wards now have toys and a nurse's duties include playing with the patients.

INDEX

Acknowledgments
Aspect Picture Library; Clive Barda; BUPA; Ron Boardman; British Diabetic Association; CNRI Institut Pasteur; Bruce Coleman; Courtauld Institute Galleries; Daily Telegraph Colour Library; Mary Evans Picture Library; Sally and Richard Greenhill; Robert Harding Associates; Michael Holford; Homeopathic Development Foundation; Homeopathic Research and Education Trust; Archivio IGDA/P Castano, C Ciccione, P Martini, G Mazza, F Arborio Mella, Pubbli-aer-Foto; Keystone Press Agency; Mansell Collection; Ken Moreman; NHPA; Mike Peters; Picturepoint; Rex Features; Science Photo Library; Ronald Sheridan; Frank Spooner Pictures; Homer Sykes; Vision International; John Watney; C James Webb; ZEFA.